A WORD ABOUT WEIGHT WATCHERS

Since 1963, Weight Watchers has grown from a handful of people to millions of enrollees annually. Today, Weight Watchers is recognized as the leading name in safe and sensible weight control. Weight Watchers members form a diverse group, from youths to senior citizens, attending meetings virtually around the globe.

Weight-loss and weight-management results vary by individual, but we recommend that you attend Weight Watchers meetings, follow the Weight Watchers food plan and participate in regular physical activity. For the Weight Watchers meeting nearest you, call 1-800-651-6000.

Weight Watchers Publishing Group
Editorial Director: Nancy Gagliardi
Senior Editor: Martha Schueneman
Associate Editor: Christine Senft, M.S.
Text: Barbara Turvett

ACKNOWLEDGMENTS

This text has been reviewed by the following members of the Weight Watchers community: Karen Miller-Kovach, M.S., R.D., General Manager of Program Development; Myron Winick, M.D., Medical Director; Michael R. Lowe, Ph.D., Member of Weight Watchers Scientific Council, Professor and Director of Clinical Training, Allegheny University for the Health Sciences; and Palma Posillico, General Manager Service Design, Training and Organizational Development. We would also like to thank Lisa R. Balick, Ph.D., Clinical Psychologist; Robert Dilts, Author/Developer; Janet Polivy, Ph.D., Professor of Psychology, University of Toronto; and James O. Prochaska, Ph.D., Director of Cancer Prevention Research Center and Professor of Psychology, University of Rhode Island; as well as the women who contributed to the comprehensive Women's Anger Study out of the University of Tennessee at Knoxville (1989–1993). We also wish to acknowledge all of the "real" people we spoke to (and there are many) about eating issues and especially those who gave us their personal stories about struggles with food and weight.

MACMILLAN
A Simon & Schuster Macmillan Company
1633 Broadway
New York, NY 10019

Copyright © 1998 by Weight Watchers International, Inc. All rights reserved.

MACMILLAN is a registered trademark of Macmillan, Inc.

WEIGHT WATCHERS is a registered trademark of Weight Watchers International, Inc.

Cataloging-in-Publication data available from the Library of Congress
ISBN 0-02-862759-8

Manufactured in the United States of America

10 9 8 7 6 5 4

Book design by Rachael McBrearty, Madhouse Studios

WEIGHT WATCHERS®

STOP STUFFING YOURSELF

7 Steps to Conquering Overeating

Macmillan • USA

Contents

Chapter 1

Why Do You Eat So Much?

It's a familiar complaint: "All my life I just wanted to eat 'normally,'" says Brenda T., 39, a public relations copywriter from the Midwest and mother of a girl. "I watched with envy the people around me who didn't seem to be ruled by food, as I was. They ate good food—as much as they seemed to want—at regular meals. If they wanted dessert, they had it, but they didn't always want it. Sometimes they had a snack, but sometimes they didn't. They didn't seem to think about food all the time, like I did; they didn't eat whenever they felt bad. Most of all, they didn't seem to struggle with their weight. Why couldn't I be like that? Why was I cursed with this war with food?"

If Brenda's words touch a chord in you, if eating and your relationship with food are in a constant struggle, know that you are not alone. The powerful allure that food and eating have over some women's lives can be unwavering and, at times, frightening. But before you spend another moment feeling inadequate and out of control, understand that you're not weak, stupid, or bad. In fact, you're probably a pretty smart, motivated, and decent person who knows that there are countless reasons why people overeat—many of them bigger and more intense than simply deciding what foods to eat or not to eat.

Things can change. It starts with understanding why you struggle with eating, then learning how to make choices for change, and finally finding ways to put them into action. But before things can change, you need to understand the complex and conflicting signals revolving around food, hunger, and eating. This chapter is designed to explain the differences between some basic physiological and psychological factors about why you eat the way you do.

The Urge to Eat: Hunger Vs. Appetite

What drives you—or anyone else—to eat? Of course, there is the biological need of all living things to stay alive with the intake of nutrients. Your body requires calories and an array of nutrients to give you energy and promote growth or maintenance (depending on your age). In the midst of this biological necessity is hunger: that gnawing feeling in your stomach when you haven't eaten in a while. Hunger is the result of your body sending a message to your brain that it requires sustenance. This message, which starts when cells are deprived of fuel (glucose), is sent through the body from neuron (nerve cell) to neuron with the help of neurotransmitters (nerve chemicals) until it reaches your brain. The brain then processes the message, and its neurons generate impulses that eventually stimulate your empty stomach to contract with hunger pangs.

True physiological hunger is often confused with appetite, which is a complex, learned response to food and the feeling of hunger. To add to the confusion, many different neurotransmitters—with names like acetylcholine, dopamine, norepinephrine, and serotonin—plus other hormonelike compounds can affect both. In addition, those who habitually eat meals at the same time each day may experience a conditioned response at each usual mealtime that feels like hunger. It may indeed be a hunger cue from the body, a signal that the body needs sustenance. It may also be an aspect of appetite that is triggered by habit conditioning, much the way Pavlov's dogs were conditioned to seek food when they heard a bell ring . . . one o'clock, time to eat.

Every time you see a commercial about luscious chocolate-chip cookies, warm and fresh from the oven, you may easily feel a desire to eat that may not be real hunger. Very purposefully, advertisers want you to respond emotionally to the visual cues they are sending. They know that your past memories of eating a delicious cookie may set off a sort of internal alarm, called sensory stimulation, that triggers you to desire the cookies at that very moment—again, conditioned response is at work here. Sometimes that alarm is designed to prompt you to eat more than you need. For instance, a certain potato chip ad constantly reminds you that you have to eat more than one. The ad's creators are suggesting that the chips are tasty while drilling into your subconscious the idea that you must eat many of them.

You can't blame your appetite—or your weight problems—entirely on the media, however. A person's eating behaviors result from an evolutionary process that starts from the moment she's born, if not before. In the early days of life, when a baby first cries out in hunger, she is comforted when her mother offers milk. The combined experience of being held, cuddled, adored, and fed is the beginning of the way she associates food with love and comfort. In fact, it is one of the first of many experiences that link emotions to hunger. Also affecting this emotional link is her genetic makeup, more specifically, how her physiology affects her weight.

Overeating and Overweight: The Chicken or the Egg?

Research in the field of obesity has skyrocketed in the past few decades. It's no wonder. With an estimated one-third of the population deemed obese (defined as 20 percent above an ideal or healthy weight from the Metropolitan Life Insurance Company height charts), unraveling the clues of how and why some people become overweight and others don't has important health and economic implications for today, as well as the future.

> ► **GENETIC FACTORS:** How many times have you thought to yourself— or heard others say about themselves—that your weight is inherited? Do you feel that no matter how much you diet the weight always comes back because it is genetically predetermined?
>
> Most people gain weight simply because their calorie consumption (or energy intake) exceeds their activity level (or energy expenditure). Yet in recent years researchers have pinpointed a so-called obesity gene in mice that controls a hormone called leptin, which tells the brain how much fat should be stored away. New research has also found that the number of taste buds you have and how sensitive they are may play a part in dictating how much of what types of food (including fat) you are prone to eat. Information about genetic makeup such as this may explain why in studies of identical twins raised apart, sets of twins were inclined

to end up around the same weight in adulthood. In other studies genetic influence appeared to affect the distribution and concentration of body fat and the amount of weight gain on a controlled diet. Also, a study of adoptees found that the subjects' adult weights more closely resembled those of their birth parents, with whom they'd had no contact, than those of their adoptive parents, with whom they had lived.

Does this mean that you are predestined to be fat? Probably not, say the researchers. But it may mean that you'll never be model skinny.

The theory about body weight "set point" adds to the genetic confusion. A set point is believed to be the individual, predetermined weight for your body. However, the research in this area has been supported by studies on animals; it is far from clear that the set-point idea is true for humans. Far better is to consider a realistic range for your weight, such as a range determined by the Body Mass Index (BMI), which is linked to both body fat and health. The range chart, on the following, is based on the BMI.

▶ CULTURAL FACTORS: Women today are savvy enough to know that society plays a pivotal role in the weight debate. The problem is that our culture—including television, movies, videos, magazines, books, even music—dictates and sends the overwhelming message that it is desirable to be thin. So even if you're a bit heavier than the weight deemed desirable for your height, you may feel fat. In response to "feeling fat," you diet, and when the diet fails or you regain the weight, you eat to soothe your anxious feelings, and the cycle of dieting and overeating repeats itself all over again.

WEIGHT WATCHERS WEIGHT RANGES

Height (feet, inches)	Weight Ranges (in pounds)			
	Minimum for All Adults	Recommended Maximum for Ages up to 25 Years	Recommended Maximum for Ages between 25 & 45	Maximum for All Adults (45+)
4'8"	89	102	107	111
4'9"	92	106	111	115
4'10"	95	110	115	119
4'11"	99	114	119	124
5'0"	102	118	123	128
5'1"	106	121	127	132
5'2"	109	125	131	136
5'3"	113	130	135	141
5'4"	116	134	140	145
5'5"	120	138	144	150
5'6"	124	142	148	155
5'7"	127	147	153	159
5'8"	131	151	158	164
5'9"	135	155	162	169
5'10"	139	160	167	174
5'11"	143	165	172	179
6'0"	147	169	177	184
6'1"	151	174	182	189
6'2"	155	179	187	194
6'3"	160	184	192	200
6'4"	164	189	197	205
6'5"	168	194	202	21

▶ **BEHAVIORAL FACTORS:** Do you often think that you can't keep weight off because you are weak and have no willpower when it comes to food? Do you feel that your emotions and behaviors concerning food play major roles in your weight problem? Interestingly, experts say that based on substantial research, emotional issues leading to problem eating are not inherent in overweight people. Rather, they are the result of cultural messages about overweight and, possibly, a side effect of stringent dieting. So does this mean you were overweight first and then became a problem eater later? Maybe.

As you can see, trying to understand if your weight problem is a result of various genetic determinants or due to a tangle of feelings and emotional reactions to cultural messages is not easy. The fact is that all of these elements probably play some sort of role in your body weight. None, however, mean you are destined to be overweight forever.

The Need to Stuff Feelings

Genetics aside, understanding the roots of your emotions and subsequent eating behavior is key to changing your habits. Most likely, your family environment was the most influential factor in how you learned to manage, express, and cope with emotions. It's also the place where you saw how to release the pressure of agitated or emotional states. Some people yell, others go for a run, while others drink to numb their feelings. And some people stuff down feelings with food.

"As a child I didn't realize it consciously, but now I see that my father was a very emotional guy," says Brenda. "He didn't often show it, but I know he had some real issues seething under the surface that he didn't know how to deal with openly. I remember seeing him sit in front of the TV most nights after dinner and down a whole bag of cookies and a quart of milk—pretty quickly too. It was like he was turning off the world with television and sweets. Boy, if that wasn't one way I learned to overeat, I don't know what was."

Humans are creatures of habit, and the habit of eating to soothe, comfort, numb emotional pain, alleviate boredom, and even celebrate happiness is learned and practiced. When habits become entrenched in your everyday life, they become normal. They are also powerful and, at times, seemingly invincible. True, old habits die hard. But habits can be broken.

Adds Brenda, "Whenever I felt out of control with food, it was a feeling, like, I have to eat; something inside of me is forcing me to do this, and I can't do anything about it. I felt I had no choice because I was so compelled to eat when I felt bad. Later on I learned that I did have choices—things I could do other than eat when the feelings were knocking at food's door. It was amazing that I could actually decide to do something else when I felt like eating. It's funny, because I consider myself to be a pretty bright person, but when I was overeating, I just couldn't figure out how to stop."

The Mystery of Memory

Family memories can be wonderful—and also tremendously telltale for understanding your habits. For instance, have you ever walked by a bakery and inhaled the aroma of fresh-baked apple pie? Even if you'd just had a meal, you probably felt "hungry" all over again. Apple pie is, of course, delicious. But the aroma is one of the most popular—and evocative: it conjures all kinds of emotion-laden memories, like Mom baking in the kitchen or family-filled holidays like Thanksgiving—a celebration solely revolving around the abundance of food and overeating.

As you go through childhood, your emotional responses to food are shaped by a variety of factors, including the way your parents themselves feel about food, the way they talk to you about it, the eating customs and traditions shaped by your ethnic heritage, the bombardment of messages you receive from the media about eating and body shape, social discrimination against those considered to be overweight, and the list goes on and on. In our society it's pretty hard to know when you really are physically hungry, because all kinds of signals stimulate your appetite all the time. Your collective experience as an individual tells the story of how you feel about food, what makes you want to eat and when, the kinds of foods you eat and how much—indeed, the extent of the influence food has on your life.

For many women, having strong feelings about food is the norm and not the exception. For centuries, in culture after culture, the connection between women and food has been powerful and undeniable. In many societies women have long been responsible for the majority of food preparation in the household. It is generally women who feed their newborn—a woman *is* food to a hungry infant—and maintain this nurturance throughout the child's early life.

To add to this, eating is and has long been a celebration in itself: a religious rite, a mode of family bonding, a centerpiece of socialization. Simply relishing the special flavors of a fine meal can send "foodies" into a state of emotional bliss. It's not surprising, then, that food and emotions are so tightly interwoven.

So Is Overeating a Disorder?

Many people who have a problem with food have come to the conclusion that there is something "wrong" with them, that they have some sort of illness. Why this kind of thinking? Well, for years experts believed that many overweight people had deep-rooted psychological problems that led to their overeating and resulting obesity. One popular self-help program has even told overeaters that they have a "disease" that they are powerless to control.

First, it is important to clarify two points:

▶ Overeating is a behavior, not a disease—either mental or physical. While overeating is a part of certain eating patterns that are considered psychiatric disorders (such as bulimia), it is not, in itself, a disorder.

▶ Obesity has recently been categorized as a medical disease; the consensus on this was supported by government-sponsored panels of experts.

In terms of emotional disorder, the research of the past two decades has turned the thinking about overeating and overweight around. Several studies conducted at the University of Pennsylvania School of Medicine suggest a clear pattern: overweight people are no more emotionally troubled than people who are not overweight. While some overeaters may have issues stemming from a troubled childhood that have spurred the misuse of food, there are many nonovereaters who are also victims of childhood abuse.

While it's true that many people who struggle with weight issues have emotional problems, the researchers conclude that these may be, not innate emotional factors, but a *result* of cultural and societal pressures about weight and thinness. In other words, a person who is perhaps genetically large may be made to feel bad about herself by messages about the desirability of thin-ness sent out by the media. She then attempts to soothe these bad feelings with food, only to exacerbate her weight issue and further her emotional issues with food. Too, the stress and depression many overeaters experience can result from frequent use of highly restrictive diets. Some researchers have found that restrained eating itself creates a condition of hyperemotionality. (Ever feel edgy, tense, or depressed while on a strict diet?) Plus, falling off a diet only to overeat or binge as a reaction to deprivation may cause feelings of hopelessness, shame, and self-loathing.

It's typical, yet ironic, that many overeaters respond to emotions by sooth-ing them with food. For various reasons that we'll examine in later chap-ters, they have learned to use food as a mechanism to deal with feelings. When this behavior is repeated time after time, it becomes such a powerful habit that it may feel like an inborn trait rather than a learned course of action.

This habitual behavior is compelling enough to make you feel as though you can't do anything to control your actions. You feel you simply must eat when you experience certain emotions, such as anger, frustration, boredom, even happiness. You think you have no choice. It's not surprising that you may feel there's something seriously wrong with your head, because at times you feel incapable of stopping the behavior.

"There were times in my life when it seemed all I did was think about food," says Brenda. "I know that's not really true, because I've always worked, had a career, had friends, been in relationships. But I remember days when every time I passed a restaurant or food stand on the street, I wanted to go in and get something to eat. Many days I'd wake up and say to myself, 'This is the day I start eating like a normal person.' But then thoughts of eating

Profile

Name: Kimberly C.
Location: Wisconsin
Age: 25
Career: Director, social work agency
Lost: 49 pounds

Kim says one of the most exciting changes in her life since losing weight has been exercise. In addition to running several miles a week, she's made small changes that make a big impact, like taking the stairs instead of the elevator whenever possible.

I have a hectic work schedule, so I'm always running to appointments, I'm always working, and I'm always late. It's a crazy lifestyle. Because of the craziness, I was eating a lot of fast food. I made really poor choices. I wasn't exercising very much. I was so stressed. In truth, I don't think I felt so great about myself.

I've had a weight problem since I was in about seventh grade. I never really tried to lose weight because I thought, "Why should I add any more stress to my life? If people don't like me for who I am, that's their problem." This was how I rationalized it, but then last year I realized that I needed to get my life under control.

My turning point involved photographs of myself. I had just been in my best friend's wedding, and when I saw the pictures, I was shocked and really quite sad: I looked gross! I realized that I was only 24 years old and had a lot going for me. I had to do something to make my health and my life better.

My mom had friends from work who had joined Weight Watchers about six months before I did, and all of them looked great, so I thought maybe it was something I could do. In fact, once I joined, they became the people who helped me stay focused. I became accountable to them, and they provided me with extra support.

I never thought that the plan would work, but it did. It truly isn't hard. In fact, my life is just as crazy and chaotic. I still don't cook very much. But now I've learned how to react to the chaos in a different way. Now if I only have time to grab fast food, I know *what* to grab when I'm going through the drive-thru. I also found out that exercise isn't so horrible. I run a few miles about twice a week.

One of the best things about my weight loss is that my health has also improved. I just feel better and I have more energy. My cholesterol has dropped, and I don't get headaches and backaches anymore. And because of the exercise, I'm not afraid to participate in physical activities anymore. In the past I thought I couldn't keep up and I would be embarrassed. At

> *Once I started losing weight, I became more self-confident. . . . I was getting attention that I never did before—and I liked it.*

least now, it's like, if I can't do it, it's because I'm a klutz . . . and that's okay! Now I have the physical stamina to do things.

Once I started losing weight, I became more self-confident. People started to look at me in a different way, so I started to dress better and feel good about myself. I was getting attention that I never did before—and I liked it.

◆ ◆ ◆

would fill up my head, and I'd overeat again. I'd keep trying, but it seemed like I couldn't stop feeling like I was controlled by food."

Bottom line: All humans have emotions and feelings, and connecting them to food need not suggest illness—mental or otherwise. Many "normal" eaters sometimes eat to help manage their feelings. Being an emotional eater doesn't mean you have a disease. Even when this link between feelings and food feels impossible to break, it's not. You can change the behavior, as many have done before. In this book we'll present several stories of women just like you who have turned their way of eating around—women who once thought they had no control over food.

An Array of Eating Behaviors

It should be noted that there are areas of troublesome behavior with food that do fall into the classification of disorder: anorexia, bulimia, and the recently defined binge eating disorder (BED). In order to understand what's what in terms of food issues, you need to understand what these terms mean and how they relate to you. *Anorexia*, in which a person actually starves herself to a point where she is dangerously underweight, and *bulimia*, in which the person repeats a pattern of gorging on large amounts of food and then compensating for the food in inappropriate ways such as vomiting, taking laxatives, fasting, or exercising excessively, are well known to the public. Recent research is suggesting that those who suffer from these disorders have a genetic predisposition to them. According to the National Eating Disorders Screening Program, 5 percent of adolescent and adult women and 1 percent of men have either anorexia, bulimia, or binge eating disorder.

Binge eating disorder (BED) was recently proposed as a new category for inclusion into the *Diagnostic and Statistical Manual of Mental Disorders,* though not on a par with anorexia and bulimia. BED is defined as the consumption of an amount of food far greater than most people would eat within an hour or two, with binges occurring at least twice a week for six months. These episodes, during which a person experiences loss of control, are not usually followed by a purge. It is estimated that as many as one to two million Americans and 10 to 15 percent of overweight people in self-help or commercial weight-loss programs (mostly women) fall into this category. As with anorexia and bulimia, BED shows up in a woman's teens or twenties, sometimes triggered by a rigid diet. Experts in the field of obesity generally recommend that anorexics, bulimics, and clinical binge eaters seek professional counseling.

Other classifications of overeaters that do not fall under the umbrella of disorders are the ones that make up the largest percentage of overweight individuals. *"Problem eaters"* are those who binge occasionally, but not as frequently as those with BED; they also do not report that feeling of extreme loss of control or other characteristics of BED, such as eating more rapidly than usual or feeling "hung over" from food the next day. *"Non-bingers"* are those who do not binge at all. They are probably the largest group of overeaters. Both problem eaters and non-bingers exhibit certain patterns of eating, including snacking, grazing, stuffing (eating consistently large meals), and less commonly, eating a majority of the day's food at night.

"I Just Want to Be a Normal Person."

Given all the factors that influence a person's eating habits, what does it mean in our society to eat "normally"? Whether you're an overeater or not, and whether you're at a comfortable weight or not, eating obviously isn't solely about physical hunger.

In addition, normal eating is not "perfect" eating. Normal eating means that you generally eat when you're hungry. Most times you eat an amount

What Type of Eater Are You?

If you're primarily a *snacker*, you probably have a busy life. You may not take the time to sit and enjoy regular meals but instead grab food on the run. You often eat a hasty breakfast or skip it altogether. You probably eat a sweet snack in the afternoon as well. The extra eating may escalate in the evening, when you're less busy and boredom, loneliness, or anxiety rises to the surface. You tend to eat while watching TV at night. Slower weekends may also be times when you reach for food several times a day.

Another form of snacking behavior seems to occur only at night. If you're a *night eater*, you probably don't feel like eating much all day. But at night, even after a good dinner, you feel the need to snack often. You may have trouble getting to sleep or staying asleep, and only food seems to help. An extreme form of this behavior, which researchers call *night eating syndrome*, is not yet categorized as a clinical eating disorder, but some experts think it should be.

If you're apt to be a *grazer*, you'll eat almost any type of food whenever and wherever it's available. You may not feel any particular emotion when you do it, but you're compelled to take food when it's around. If you're a *stuffer*, you probably eat at regular mealtimes. But most of your meals are large enough to make you feel very full, very often.

You may see yourself in one of these patterns. Habitual eating behaviors become so much a part of daily life that they can be difficult to recognize and even more difficult to understand. In the next chapter our "emotional eating quiz" will help you to see your troublesome eating patterns and habits more clearly so you can take steps to change them.

of food that makes you feel satisfied, but not stuffed. You may regularly eat three times a day, twice a day, or six times a day. You might eat the same thing for breakfast every day, or you might not. Whatever the pattern, it feels comfortable to you. It means you often choose foods that you know will give your body what it needs, but sometimes you'll eat food just for the sheer pleasure of it. Ultimately, normal eating means that there are other thoughts that occupy your day besides those of food.

But there is a surprising part: Normal eating means you might have an extra snack sometimes, you might eat a rich dessert, you might even eat to calm your nerves occasionally. It means you have food cravings and you satisfy them when you need to with small amounts. Sometimes you will eat a large meal, but you probably will feel like eating less at the next meal. You might overeat at family gatherings or you might not. You enjoy the taste, smell, and texture of food, but sometimes you eat in a hurry without much pleasure. Some days you won't even care about eating, but you'll eat because your body is "asking" for fuel. You might even skip a meal if you have no appetite or if you're very busy. *While your history and your lifestyle affect your eating habits and patterns, food does not rule your life.*

What the Experts Say, What Overeaters Say

The research community has changed its collective mindset many times about why people overeat. In 1989, Richard M. Ganley reviewed 30 years of studies on eating and emotion, concluding that overweight people reported a much higher degree of emotional eating than nonoverweight people and this eating helped them to reduce feelings such as anger, depression, loneliness, boredom, and anxiety.

Extra! Extra!

You may have read about research suggesting that an imbalance in some nerve chemicals, such as dopamine or serotonin, or other hormone-like compounds, causes food cravings in some people. For example, according to studies at the Massachusetts Institute of Technology, serotonin affects our central nervous system by easing tension and enhancing concentration. In most of us, our body's serotonin level is stable throughout the day. But for some people the level drops in the afternoon. The result, as reported by many in weight-control programs, is feelings of stress and tension and an urge to eat carbohydrates, including sugar. Why carbohydrates? Because, the research suggests, for some people they help the brain produce more serotonin. This suggests that some food cravings may be biologically induced. Not all researchers in this field buy into this theory, but the possibility could account for the reason so many experience a late-afternoon lull and hunger.

While we're on the subject of cravings, if you're a woman there's a one in two chance that you crave chocolate, according to a University of Michigan study. A variety of research into why this is so points to some of chocolate's ingredients: the stimulants caffeine and theobromine, which can give you a lift; the chemical phenylethylamine, which may replicate a feeling of being in love; the fat, which may cause a release of feel-good endorphins in your brain; and the sugar, which stimulates serotonin production and its resultant feeling of calm. As with the serotonin-carbohydrate connection, the research is inconclusive as to whether our body is really asking us to eat this substance. But few can argue that the cravings are real and powerful.

Yet in 1993 David B. Allison and Stanley Heshka at St. Luke's-Roosevelt Hospital's Obesity Research Center in New York City suggested that Ganley's research was flawed. Their study concluded that often overweight people overreport emotional eating as a result of a societal expectation to do so. They learn what's expected of them in therapy and may alter their own thinking to "please" the therapist.

Still, clinical psychologists who treat people with eating issues assert that emotional eating is a major and very real problem for many of their patients. Overeaters who talk about their issues in support groups and at self-help program meetings say passionately and often that they are eating in response to all kinds of emotions.

Ultimately, you must look inside yourself and decide what's true. Millions of people who seek help from private or group therapy, who join weight-management support programs, and who seek the counsel of understanding friends and loved ones report varying degrees of eating to manage feelings. These eating patterns can be powerful and may at times seem impossible to alter. But what is just as powerful is the knowledge that feelings can be managed in other ways and that situations that trigger you to overeat can be altered or avoided.

It's not always easy to make these kind of changes in your life. Feelings are scary, and allowing yourself to feel them instead of immediately reaching for food to mask them is a daunting choice. At first it can be very painful. But you probably know that overeating and its consequences can also be very painful. When you discover what it is that makes you eat too much and then learn techniques for changing your behavior that really work, you're on your way to enjoying eating—and your life—in a way you didn't think was possible. You can break the cycle, the deep-rooted habit of using food to manage your emotions, with understanding, information, and practice.

Chapter 2

Discovering Your Eating Style

"*I* *was 16 when I first went on a diet," says Rhonda R.,*
a 44-year-old financial portfolio manager in New York City. "At
that time I was 12 pounds heavier than I thought I should be for my
5'0" height. I wanted to take diet pills, but my mother wouldn't let
me. So she sent me to Weight Watchers instead. Before I went there, I
was clueless about what made me eat more than I should. But at the
meetings I learned that some people eat in response to emotions. Boy,
did that hit home. It was like a lightbulb went off in my head. 'I do
that.' I ate when I met a guy I liked and was disappointed when he
didn't call me. I ate when I was nervous about a school test. I also
ate when I wanted to celebrate something, say, with my mom. I knew
I was eating over feelings, but I didn't know what to do about it. It
was a problem, but I didn't know how to solve it."

Problem solving. It's something you learn about, ideally, at an early age. You learn that when you need to work on a problem, whether it's part of a school lesson, a project at your job, or a situation at home, it helps to look at the problem in terms of sections. You learn to break the complex problem down into manageable pieces that can be understood and addressed individually. Then you can put the pieces back together to find the overall solution.

The problem of overeating is no different. You know it's a problem that is made up of a number of factors:

▶ It's about the food itself—what you like and don't like, what you crave, what satisfies you, the eating choices you make.

▶ It's about how much you eat—whether you eat small amounts often, large amounts less often, whether you eat more when you're bored and less when you're busy or whether being too busy makes you want more food.

▶ It's about your attitudes—about the way you eat, about your weight, and about your body size and shape.

▶ It's about your emotional connection to food—what feelings and events trigger eating, how these triggers came to be, and how you feel after you eat.

Figuring out what these factors are, however, so that you can understand and deal with each one can be confusing. For example, you may have already learned, as Rhonda did, that you respond to certain feelings by eating. What you may not know is what feelings and situations trigger eating and to what extent. You may get the urge to eat from only one or two different emotions, or you may eat over every emotional experience. You may feel compelled to soothe intense feelings with food, but not gentle ones. Sometimes you may have vague, floating feelings that you soothe with food, feelings that you can't quite put your finger on.

"When I first went to Weight Watchers in the '60s, hardly anyone was talking about eating over emotional issues," explains Rhonda. "I see now that the fact that Weight Watchers even suggested this was really something. But I did not, at the time, learn how to deal with the feelings in ways other than eating. So over the course of 24 years, I lost weight and gained weight and lost and gained, and with all of this came more bad feelings about myself that led to more eating. Every time I felt an overwhelming urge to eat, I thought, 'Here I go again.' I felt out of control, guilty, and angry. I didn't realize it then, but in retrospect I see that my self-esteem plummeted as my eating problem and weight escalated. Eventually I think I ate over every feeling I had."

It's not always easy to remember, after the fact, what feelings and situations spurred eating episodes. That's why, in addition to taking the quiz that follows, you'll want to keep a week's log or diary of the times and places you eat, what you eat, and how you feel before and after eating.

At the end of your week, review the feelings, people, places, and times that affect your eating, as well as the types and amounts of food you eat. Take note of the emotions, situations, and patterns that repeat. You'll then have more information about your particular triggers and your responses to them. This diary will be very personal and sensitive, but remember that no one will see this but you, and the things you'll learn from it will help you tremendously.

As you read the following chapters, your quiz answers and the notes in your diary will become more and more revealing. You'll gain a greater understanding of those things that might, at first, seem surprising or unclear. You'll see the pieces of your eating profile come together as if you were completing a jigsaw puzzle. You'll relate to some of the issues covered in the book perfectly, others somewhat, others perhaps not at all. You'll be able to choose the specific tips and strategies that can help you solve your own issues. Finally, you'll have a complete understanding of your eating behavior. Then you can use the methods for change discussed in Chapter Nine to really turn your life around.

Your Eating Profile

Answer the questions in this three-part quiz as accurately as possible. Think about each question for a moment or two before you respond. Remember that there are no right or wrong answers. They should not be based on how you *think* you should feel or behave. You do, however, need to look inside yourself to find your own truth. It's likely that you won't be sure about some of the feelings and situations described in the questions. Just answer the best that you can and don't worry if you're not certain.

Take all three parts of the quiz first. Then read the scoring guides at the end of each section to learn about your primary issues.

Each of the questions in all sections will have five answer choices: 1. Never, 2. Rarely, 3. Occasionally, 4. Often, 5. Always. Choose one answer for each, and write the corresponding number, from 1 to 5, next to each question.

PART ONE: *Feeding Feelings*

1. When you get mad at someone, including yourself, do you get the urge to eat?

2. Do you reach for a snack or head for the refrigerator when you feel annoyed?

3. If someone or something disappoints you, do you feel like eating?

4. When you're ticked off all day, do you eat more than usual?

5. Do you gravitate toward food when you're bored?

6. Do you comfort feelings of loneliness by eating?

7. If you feel restless, is food the first thing you think of to calm yourself?

8. Is food your friend when you feel empty inside or unloved?

9. Do you ease feelings of stress by munching?

10. Does eating help soothe you when life seems overwhelming?

11. Are big changes in your life followed by weight gain?

12. Does worry cause you to eat more than usual?

13. Do you ever say to yourself, "I'm fat anyway, I may as well eat"?

14. Do you ever eat to punish yourself?

15. Do you ever eat to reward yourself?

16. Does a general feeling of agitation cause you to snack?

17. When you're feeling moody, do you feel like eating?

18. Do you crave extra food when you have "the blues"?

19. When you're anxious and you don't know why, do you eat to take the edge off?

20. Do you eat more when you feel excited?

21. Do you overeat when you celebrate?

PART ONE: *Scoring and Interpretation*

Add up the numbers of the answers for all 21 questions. If, for instance, your answer to a question is 4—often—give yourself 4 points for that question. A total score of 77 or more suggests that you regularly eat to manage feelings and emotions. If some groups of questions seem to have higher scores than others, it may indicate that one or more specific emotional states push you to eat.

▶ If your answers to the first four questions are mostly 4s and 5s, you probably eat to stuff down **anger**. Because, even today, society teaches women that anger is not an appropriate or acceptable emotion to express, many women suppress it, often by calming angry feelings with food. To learn about how anger affects you, how you deal with it, and other ways to manage it besides eating, see Chapter Seven.

▶ If your answers to questions 5 through 8 are mostly 4s and 5s, you tend to reach for food when you are **bored** or feel **lonely**. Many people see food as a friend. So it's no surprise that they turn to it when they feel lonely or unloved. Boredom, like loneliness, is the result of isolation—from people and/or stimulating activity—and for many, food alleviates the tedium. In Chapter Eight you'll find out how to handle loneliness and boredom with actions other than eating.

▶ If your answers to questions 9 through 12 are mostly 4s and 5s, **stressful** events or times in your life promote your overeating. Even people who don't generally eat in response to other feelings will reach for extra food to ease stress. If a big project at work, a move to a new home, or simply a period when there's just that much more to do leads you to calm yourself with food, see Chapter Six to understand this behavior and find alternatives for it.

▶ If your answers to questions 13 through 15 are mostly 4s and 5s, your **body image** and **self-esteem** need a boost. Considering the long-standing social pressure for women to be thin, it's no wonder that so many feel inadequate when it comes the size and shape of their body. Poor body image in turn leads to feelings of low self-worth, and both lead many to food for comfort. Chapter Four will help you see how eating is tied to your image of yourself and how to break the "I'm fat anyway, I'll eat" cycle.

▶ If your answers to questions 16 through 19 are mostly 4s and 5s, your **day-to-day moods**, some of which result from the hormonal fluctuations of your cycle, urge you to munch. Many women report that they just can't stop eating when they're premenstrual, for example. Some get overwhelming cravings for carbohydrates and sweets at certain times of the month. If mood fluctuations rule your food, read Chapter Five so you can be aware and ready to take care of yourself in ways other than eating.

PART TWO: *The Way You Eat*

1. Do you usually eat at the same mealtimes each day?

2. Do you think your meals are very large?

3. Do you like to feel very full after eating?

4. Do you reach for food whenever it's available?

5. Do you eat most any food that's around?

6. Do you snack in between regular meals?

7. Do you crave sweet snacks?

8. Do you skip breakfast?

9. Do you eat a small lunch or skip lunch altogether?

10. Do you need a snack in the afternoon?

11. Do you eat a lot at night?

12. Do you need to eat to help you sleep?

13. Do you eat large amounts of food in the course of an hour or two?

14. Do you "zone out" when you eat?

15. Do you eat whole bags of cookies or chips or whole containers of ice cream at one time?

PART TWO: *Scoring and Interpretation*

This section of the quiz is designed to help you see any patterns in your eating behavior. Many people don't realize when, how much, and what kinds of food they're consuming during a day because their particular hand-to-mouth behavior becomes an almost unconscious habit. When you recognize your eating style—whether you graze, snack, stuff, binge, or have overlapping patterns—you can use the knowledge, along with what you learn about your emotional and situational triggers, to alter your eating in a way that's comfortable and "normal" for you.

> ▶ If your answers to the first three questions are mostly 4s and 5s, you're a **stuffer**. This is probably the most clearcut pattern of overeating and maybe the simplest to deal with. You already have set mealtimes; you need to work on portion control and get in touch with the comfort of feeling satisfied without being stuffed. People who need to feel overly full are often those who want to keep many feelings from surfacing. This book will help you recognize this behavior in yourself and show you how you can live through your feelings without overeating.

> ▶ If your answers to questions 4 and 5 are 4s or 5s, you're a **grazer**. You reach for food whenever it's available, and you may not be aware of—or even care—what, where, and how much you're eating. Knowing that this is your pattern will help raise your consciousness about your eating habits so you can make decisions about food choices based on taste and preference, and set specific times for eating that will work for your lifestyle. This kind of nonspecific overeating may be a reaction to gen-

eral stress and anxiety. Chapter Six and possibly Chapter Five will help you deal with constant grazing behavior.

▶ If your answer to questions 6 through 10 are mostly 4s and 5s, you're a **snacker**. There are probably certain times and places that you go for extra food each day that part three of this quiz will help you identify. Boredom and loneliness are often triggers for this pattern. If this is so for you, pay particular attention to Chapter Eight.

▶ If your answers to questions 8 through 12 are mostly 4s and 5s, you're a **night eater**. If you can answer all of these questions with mostly 5s, you may suffer from **night eating syndrome.** Your anxieties surface in the evening, and you need to understand this and find other ways to calm and relax yourself besides eating. It also helps to set up regular mealtimes so that hunger at night doesn't add to the emotional issues as a cause of overeating. Most night eaters eat alone. Chapter Eight can help.

▶ If your answers to questions 13 through 15 are mostly 4s and 5s, you're a **binger**. If you've been bingeing, you're most likely seeking relief from some intense emotions, maybe anger, guilt, or extreme anxiety. You need to focus on these underlying emotional issues and deal with them first. Pay close attention to the information in Chapters Four and Seven.

PART THREE: *People, Places, and Food*

1. Do you snack a lot at work?

2. Do you reach for food after confrontations with your boss or co-workers?

3. Do you keep sweets in your desk drawer?

4. Do you reward yourself after housework with food treats?

5. Do you snack a lot around your kids?

6. Do you taste a lot while you cook?

7. Do you snack while watching TV?

8. Do you eat more around your husband than otherwise?

9. Do you eat more when you feel you don't get enough sex?

10. Do you think you avoid sex by overeating or gaining weight?

11. Does a phone conversation with your mother end with you reaching for a snack?

12. Do you eat more when you're at your parents' for dinner?

13. Do family get-togethers inspire you to eat large amounts of food?

14. Do you eat in your car?

15. Do you snack while running errands?

16. Do you tend to eat when you're alone?

17. Do you and your friends plan activities primarily around food and meals?

18. Do you eat a lot in social situations, such as parties or sports events?

PART THREE: *Scoring and Interpretation*

▶ If your answers to the first three questions are mostly 4s or 5s, aspects of your job are triggering problem eating. Many women report eating more and gaining weight during periods of cranked-up work stress. Chapter Six can help you understand and deal with eating on the job.

▶ If your answers to questions 4 through 7 are mostly 4s or 5s, some of your eating issues are connected to your feelings about **housework, home,** and **family.** Reactions to boredom, tedium, and low self-worth come into play here. In addition, you may have learned certain home eating behaviors from your mother. See Chapters Three, Four and Eight.

▶ If your answers to questions 8 through 10 are mostly 4s or 5s, you may have underlying issues in your **relationship** (which may in-clude sexual tension) that are leading you to overeat. Sometimes the comfort of a good marriage can lead to overeating as well. You need to learn to separate eating from feelings about sex and your partner. A better sense of your own identity, which is addressed in Chapter Four, can help.

▶ If your answers to questions 11 through 13 are mostly 4s or 5s, you have a hard time separating **family** and food, as do many people. The influence of your parents and of cultural heritage has a long and strong arm. Plus, if one or both parents had a problem with overeating, you may have picked up the message. Chapter Three is devoted to these and many other family ties to food.

▶ If your answers to questions 14 through 16 were 4s or 5s, you're a solo snacker. Many people eat, and eat too much, in **isolation**, sometimes out of shame or embarrassment, sometimes just because it's comfortable to be alone with food. Problems with body image, loneliness, or boredom contribute to this behavior. To find out how to break this habit, focus on Chapters Four and Eight.

▶ If your answers to questions 17 and 18 are 4s or 5s, you overdo the food thing in **social** situations. You may just like to party hearty, or it's possible that you feel "less than" when with friends and push down the bad feeling with extra food. Chapters Three and Four will help you modify this behavior.

After the Quiz

Congratulations. By answering these questions honestly, you've taken a big step to understanding your individual problem-eating triggers. You may have found that you experience many of these issues or only one or two. If just about all of them apply to you, you shouldn't feel strange. So many of the feelings, patterns, and situations that trigger overeating are interconnected. Many people who struggle with food and weight report that they overeat for all kinds of reasons in all kinds of circumstances.

Does that mean you have to have a separate solution for every issue? Not necessarily. A strategy to deal with one aspect may well help with others. Remember, the overall task is to change problem-eating behavior by understanding it, learning about alternative behaviors, and taking the steps to change it.

"My life is about making choices now," says Rhonda. "I still get urges to eat over feelings, but I know now that when I want to eat a whole other meal right after I've already eaten one, there's other stuff going on. It's not about hunger. Now I know I can do other things instead of eat. I didn't know that before. When that chocolate calls to me, I choose to call a friend instead of eating chocolate. It's just not worth it to me to go back to my old behavior, to give in to the food urges. I feel too good now."

◆

Chapter ③

Family: The Root of All Eating?

"*From as far back as I can remember, I was the eater in the family,*" *says Linda M., a singer and actress of Italian heritage who hails from the Boston area.* "*My older sister never ate much, so my grandmother always turned to me to eat the leftover food at the table—'Linda, finish this,' or 'Linda, eat the rest of that.' They knew that 'garbage gut' here would finish everything. And I did. I liked eating a lot, and I was mostly very obedient. I didn't want to make waves.*"

It probably won't surprise you to hear that your eating habits and the way your emotions come into play when you eat began taking shape at an early age. The family dinner table is a breeding ground for food behaviors that can last a lifetime. Not only do the food traditions and mores of your heritage have their "say" here, but family members' individual and collective attitudes about eating and weight invariably affect the temperament of mealtimes. Your earliest memories probably include activities around food.

And why not? Most likely you associate food with the comfort and love, or perhaps the lack of it, that you received from your family during childhood.

The point of this chapter is to help you understand how your family and heritage contribute to your eating behavior so you can take steps to change the behaviors that don't work for you. This is not to say that everything you gleaned from your family about food and eating is bad and made things difficult for you. Sure, you have issues with food. If you didn't, you probably wouldn't be reading this book. But as you go through this chapter, remember that along with any problem habits that took root in your childhood are the many pleasures and joys associated with meals, cooking, tasting, eating, and socialization that were shaped in your youth with your family's help.

And it goes back even further.

The Birth of Eating

The first time you as a human being came into contact with food was, of course, the first day of your life. As a newborn, you had a biological need to be fed and nurtured, and most likely your mother responded to your hunger cries by giving you milk. At the same time, she held you in her arms and offered comfort and love. This is an important moment—when food, love, and comfort are first tied together.

If a mother regularly responds appropriately to an infant's cries for food, the child will most likely begin to learn what the sensation of hunger is and how that sensation should be answered. If the baby's biological need to eat is regularly met with the offer of food, she should develop a sense that it is appropriate to eat when she feels hunger and, in turn, appropriate to stop eating when she feels satisfied and no longer hungry. As the child grows into adulthood, there's a good chance she will learn to feed herself in the same manner. She will intrinsically trust herself for the right kind of nurturance, just as she learned to trust her parent when she was a baby.

But what happens when a mother often responds inappropriately to a baby's needs? Some experts believe that when a parent neglects an infant's need for food or, by contrast, overindulges the child with constant offers of food to soothe needs other than hunger, the child may grow up confused about what hunger really is and the way to satisfy it. A child whose need for food has been neglected may grow up with a need to reach for extra food later in life, just as a child who has often been soothed with food may later overeat to comfort herself.

Overall, to a baby, being fed means being loved. That most people carry this link into adulthood is not surprising. "I love food." "Food is my best friend." "A great meal is better than great sex." Most likely, you've heard or said phrases such as these often. They clearly indicate the long-lasting power of the food-love connection that has its beginnings in the first days of life.

Growing Up at the Table

Learning, including the shaping of attitudes and behaviors, is an ongoing process, and your eating education is no exception. What starts in infancy as a simple lesson of eating to satisfy hunger becomes a more complicated process as you begin to understand the verbal and nonverbal signals about food put out by your family members.

For example, a mother's preoccupation with food and weight may play a significant role in the way she feeds her young child and also in the early messages that child receives from her about eating. A telling Yale University study of mothers and one-year-olds of "normal" weight, conducted by Judith Rodin, Ph.D., and Stephen Reznick, Ph.D., shows differences in how mothers with varying concerns about their own weight act while feeding their babies. The mothers who were highly preoccupied with weight issues were erratic in their behavior during the meals, sometimes urging their toddlers to eat more, sometimes restricting the amount of food, sometimes rushing feedings. These mothers showed a much greater display of emotional arousal while feeding their babies than did mothers who were less concerned about their weight. It is probable that babies are highly susceptible to the kind of emotional cues they receive from their mothers during meals.

Some of the first power struggles between a young child and her parents take place at mealtimes. A toddler has very little control over her young life and soon finds that one way to exert control is by managing her own food. She may display power by throwing food, refusing to eat, or demanding more food and then not eating it. Parents' reactions to these little power ploys send various messages to their child. If, for instance, the parents become very agitated during these episodes, the child may learn that eating truly can be a way to gain power and control. As this child grows to adulthood, she may learn to use food and the way she eats as a coping mechanism when she feels powerless (some adults who feel out of control think that, at times, food is the only thing in their life that they *can* control). If, however, the parents remain calm and show that the child's food tactics are no big deal, the child learns that power is not about food, and vice versa.

Food and power issues often occur as a child gets older, and sometimes it's the parents who try to exert the control. How many times did your parent say to you something like "You can't go out to play unless you drink all your milk"? Some other ways parents use food as a ploy:

▶ As a reward—"If you do all your homework we'll go for an ice-cream sundae."

▶ For comfort—"Eat this pudding, you'll feel better." (Can you remember your mother ever saying, "Go out and exercise, you'll feel better" or "Go read a book, you'll feel better"?)

▶ As punishment—"You have to sit at the dinner table until you eat all your vegetables."

▶ As a guilt trip—"Eat what's on your plate; children are starving all over the world."

Statements and attitudes such as these serve to confuse the issue of what food is about for a child. It's all too common to carry these messages into adulthood, when they may have a telling influence on how a person relates to food. You may have developed the habit of always eating whatever is in front of you, whether you're hungry or not, as a member of the "clean plate club." Likewise, if the comfort angle was played out to the extreme in your family, you might have the recurring habit of trying to make yourself feel better—whether the discomfort is physical or emotional—with food. In Linda's case, it was a combination of two strong food connections, food as comfort and food as love, that triggered some very troublesome eating behaviors.

"My mother always said, 'We can't afford this or that, but you always have food on the table and clothes on your back.' This was her big thing. We could, and should, always eat even when we couldn't do or have other things. That was her way of loving us. No hugs, no kisses, but food on the table. Not much affection, lots of food.

"I remember, starting back when I was 10 or 11, afternoons when I came home from school, when my mother would have spaghetti sauce made and give us lists of our chores and then go to work. My sister was out somewhere playing, my father wasn't home yet, my grandmother was downstairs. I would take out the sauce and cook spaghetti and eat it before dinner. Then I'd clean everything up so no one would know what I'd done. Afterward I guess I felt guilty. That's why I cleaned everything up and left no trace. I ate in secret. Then I'd have a regular dinner with the family. I think I did it because I was lonely and got very little attention. Somehow it had already happened that food was my sole comfort. I just didn't get the comfort I needed from my mom or dad."

It's not just the things parents say that influence your food behavior. A family rife with tensions often plays out its drama around the dinner table, at the time of day when the whole family is together. A child may watch her parents argue, or feel the stress of an angry silence, and those knots in her stomach become mixed up with her hunger and the impulse to eat. Some children may grow up eating less as a result; some may grow up eating more to calm that stressful feeling.

"Traditionally, Italian family Sunday dinners are big happy meals with the whole family, but for us they were horrible," says Linda. "We had a big hot meal nearly every night. Then on Sunday my grandmother would prepare the sauce, and we all would prepare for a big dinner with the pasta and everything. And then my mother and sister would have a big fight and my mother would lock herself in her room, and my father would tell her to come on down to dinner and she wouldn't come. And the rest of us would be sitting around the table stressed to the max. That happened almost every weekend. I remember that so well. Sunday dinners were always stressful for us. But I always ate everything anyway. I still eat big meals. I have to sit down and have a hot meal for dinner, no matter what. And I have to eat a lot or I don't feel satisfied."

You Are (Partly) What Your Parents Eat

Kids have to learn eating habits from someone, and most likely they'll pick up most of them from their parents—which can be good or not so good. If a parent overeats, eats very fast, snacks a lot, or eats in front of the television, a child may learn the very same behavior and carry it into adulthood. If you watched your mother get angry and then eat instead of expressing it, you may do that too. Do you eat to try to ease stress? Many people do, as did their parents.

When one or both parents are overeaters, a child may learn just by watching that it's "okay" to overeat. Some parents encourage—whether consciously or not—their children to overeat as a way to legitimize their own misuse of food, and often in the name of love. If one or both of your parents was overweight and alternately ate a lot, went on a diet, fell off the diet, and returned to overeating, chances are that behavior had an influence on your adult eating patterns.

The types of foods your parents ate affect what you eat. Linda grew up in a family where meat, potatoes, and especially pasta were the foods of choice. To this day these foods make up her dinners. She adds, "Fruit was a big thing in our family. Sweets were only there for holidays and company. And for me still, if I had to give up something, sweets would be it."

A taste for less-than-healthy foods can be the result of growing up with these foods in the house. Your parents may have consumed heavy meat meals, fried foods, rich desserts, and chips and cookies as steady staples of their diet. You're smart enough to know that most of these foods are high in fat and calories, but you may still be prone to reaching for them regularly. That's because many food preferences are habits that are formed early and become a part of your "normal" adult behavior. In addition, the foods you learned to think of as "treats" in your childhood, such as candy, pizza, ice-cream sodas, and the like, may be the ones you now think of as "bad" or "forbidden" foods. These are the kinds of foods people tend to go off their diets for—the ones they feel deprived without.

For some, eating the way their parents did is a way of showing allegiance to them. They mirror their parents' behavior and hold on to it as a subconscious expression of love and loyalty. Giving up this behavior can symbolize leaving parents or even betraying them in some way. An extreme yet related scenario involves a girl with anorexia who, in a sense, keeps herself from growing up by forcing her body to remain small and childlike. In this way she doesn't have to become an adult and leave her parents. Sometimes anorexic behavior is a means of taking care of parents. A girl whose parents have a troubled relationship feels that her actions are perhaps holding them together or that she is keeping their secrets in some way with her secretive behavior.

Mom, Dad, and Me (The Chubby One)

Researchers generally agree that young children are better at their own food regulation than are older children or adults. Studies show that when they're fed more than usual at one meal or snack time, kids will usually compensate by eating less at the next, and vice versa. They'll eat enough and get the right amount of activity to support their natural weight tendencies.

The problem, some experts believe, is when parents try to control their child's food intake. Our societal yearning for thinness not only propels adults into dieting but may also be responsible for concerned parents putting a plump child on a diet of sorts. While this intention to help the child reach a "normal" weight may seem well-meaning, it can be problematic for the child. Kids whose eating habits are overregulated by their parents are not as able to adjust their own eating according to whether they are hungry or satisfied. They are the ones who will eat that afternoon snack even when they've had a very large lunch.

The many ways that parents try to control their child's eating behavior can make it difficult for the child to retain her innate sense of internal food regulation. Any child who is put on some sort of diet may lose the ability to know what real hunger is. Her natural ability to regulate her own weight can become skewed. Plus, some children become rebellious when forced to restrict food. They then eat favorite foods behind their parents' backs—another habit that can easily be carried into adulthood.

It's perfectly natural for parents to want to help their child maintain a comfortable and healthy body weight. If, according to her physician, a child is gaining too much weight for her height, the optimal way for parents to help is to encourage the child to eat healthier, lower-fat foods and engage in more physical activity. The key is not to force dieting but to encourage a healthier lifestyle.

Another way a child learns to eat more than she needs is when she becomes the designated "fat one" in the family. Some parents, unaware of the potentially deleterious consequences of their actions, put their children into niches with labels: "my cute one," "my smart one," "the brat," "my rebellious kid," "the chubby one." This is what happened to Linda. When her sister refused to eat but she complied, her family made a habit of urging her to

Profile

Name: Alexandra S.

Location: New York

Age: 25

Career: Editor

Lost: 84 pounds

Alexandra varies her workouts by taking spinning and dance classes, in addition to running three miles four times a week.

I was always on the heavy side as a child, but once I got to high school, I started eating a *lot*. Then, when I was 16, my mother died and I *really* started to overeat. I was always heavy (I've been overweight since I was about eight years old), but after she died, I gained 40 pounds. Looking back, I don't remember how I coped. I think I just denied her death. I tried to continue going on with my life like nothing had happened. It wasn't until a full year later that I realized I'd gained all that weight.

Right after my mom died, I was pretty much in a daze. The way I would eat after she died, I wouldn't be tasting it or enjoying it. I would just be stuffing food in my mouth. Now I realize that I wasn't even hungry. I didn't connect to the fact that I was eating in reaction to emotions.

I also wasn't going out with guys, and all of my friends had boyfriends. On weekends I stayed home, watched movies, and ate. I was into snacking—I'd munch on M&M's and ice cream. One incident that really stands out in my memory was one day at the beach with a bunch of friends. I pretended that I forgot something so I could go back to the house. Once I got there, I ate a whole row of fudge-covered cookies! When someone asked who did it, I didn't say anything. I remember thinking I didn't want anyone to see me eating like that. I was totally out of control.

I started to lose weight my sophomore year in college because I fell in love. Until then I had always eaten in reaction to situations that upset me. If a family member criticized my weight, I would start eating. I did that all the time. Now I realize that I wasn't even hungry, but if I was upset, I would say, "Okay, I'm going to go get ice cream," and then I'd feel better.

I've never been good at expressing my anger. I hold things in—but I'm working on it. Now, instead of eating, I tell myself to do something else. I make myself go to the gym or write in my journal. It's still something I have to work on. For instance, after I once had a fight with my boyfriend, I didn't eat, even though I wanted to. I went to the gym instead. Also, I try to minimize the damage. Instead of saying, "I'm feeling bad, I'm going to get ice cream," I get frozen yogurt. I figure I'm at least trying to improve a bad habit.

I also carry a picture of myself when I was heavier. I refuse to look like that again. I pull it out when I need some motivation. For example, I once went five days without working out. On the

"It took me joining Weight Watchers 11 times before I was successful—I finally proved I could do it."

sixth day I thought, "What's one more day?"; then I pulled out the picture. Just seeing it made me go.

The best advice I can give someone who is trying to lose weight is to let it out, whether you have to go into a room and yell or write in a journal. I come from a family in which you don't express your emotions, and I just don't think that's healthy. You have to find the techniques and strategies that are helpful and healthy for you. My advice is just to do it.

eat the leftovers, knowing she would. In this way her parents and grand-mother had at least one child who would obey their authority. They felt grati-fied by this, and she, as the chosen fat sister, learned to eat too much as a way to show her love and loyalty—and to avoid the difficult confrontations she saw her older sister and parents enact.

Does Sibling Rivalry Make You Eat?

"I've always resented my sister for her thinness," says Linda. "People always said to her as a child, 'Janet, you're so thin, you should eat more.' Then they'd look at me as if to say, 'You should stop eating.' Plus, my mother would dress us in matching outfits. I'd see pictures of us in which Janet looked tall and thin, and I looked short and squat. I really resented her, even more so when she'd say, 'I wish people would stop saying how thin I am.'"

To this day, says Linda, she feels a rivalry with her sister that had its roots at the family dinner table. It's not surprising to hear that sibling rivalry may be wrapped around food, eating, weight concerns, and appearance. Studies show that girls become body conscious at an early age and that many have been on a diet by age 10. A scenario involving sisters comparing how much they are eating or not eating, how many hours they can go without eating, or how long they can go without any sweets is not hard to imagine. You may have experienced something like this yourself.

These kinds of food dramas are exactly the kind that can take hold and sustain into adulthood, influencing the way you eat and feel about food. For some, just seeing a sister can trigger all sorts of feelings about food that began at home in childhood. And these feelings can trigger overeating.

Ties That Bind

You may not have lived with your parents or other family members for some time. You may not even see them that often. But oh, how their reach can take you by the hand and lead you to the food. "Just like when I was a kid with my family, I'm still not very good at confronting other people when I have an issue with them," admits Linda. "And I still don't like hearing anyone else argue either. I'm better now, but I still want to eat instead of confronting anyone or anything. Eating is my comfort."

If a phone conversation with your mom ends with you heading straight for the refrigerator, you shouldn't feel stupid or weak. Many women report that their mothers have a way of triggering feelings that lead to overeating. Remember that the beginnings of your relationship with her were all tied up in the way she fed, comforted, and nurtured you. Consider how her messages to you about food when you were a child may connect with the way you can get agitated after even a simple chat with her today. That's powerful stuff.

Even when you've made a serious effort to eat healthier foods and smaller portions than you learned to eat growing up, a weekend at the folks' house can be a weekend of eating regression. Those old, familiar surroundings, those memories, those old smells, that old wallpaper, the sound of your father's voice—all these things can trigger that old way of eating. A family holiday gathering can mean celebrating with a lot of food for several days. It can also mean stuffing yourself to ease the tensions of family dynamics.

No one can trigger the intense emotions that lead to overeating more effectively than the people with whom you grew up. If you felt that you could never please your parents, or you constantly strove to outdo your mother or a sibling, being with these family members can cause these old issues to come raging back. One former compulsive eater admits that she moved to a new town partly to get away from her sister. "I used to feel so angry around her. She really knew how to push my buttons, and it really contributed to my food abuse. For a while, every time I'd see her I'd feel the same way and lapse into old habits. But now all the work has paid off. I don't eat because I'm angry about my sister anymore."

Your Heritage and Your Food

Whether your background is Italian, Chinese, Jewish, Greek, African American, Hispanic, or just about any other ethnicity, you most likely have food preferences and habits that have been shaped by your heritage. You'd be hard-pressed to find a nationality that did not have its food and cooking rituals. Bookstores are filled with cookbooks extolling the cuisines of hundreds of countries and their various regions. A few examples of cultural influence on eating:

- ▶ In Pakistan many foods are hot and highly spiced, so a dessert of cool and sweet items usually follows to soothe heated tongues and stomachs. (Do you get the urge to eat a sweet after every meal?)

- ▶ In Italy the word *abondanza* describes the main meal—large platters of fresh meats, pastas, vegetables, fruits, and cheeses are served "family style." (Do you feel unsatisfied unless you eat really big meals?)

- ▶ In France meals are taken very seriously, and it's not unusual to be at the dinner table for a few hours.

There are any number of social rituals and rites tied to food in many cultures. Most holidays include some sort of feast, often with special foods; funerals and wakes often include eating as part of the event; even religious rites of various cultures include food and drink. With such important activities intertwined with eating in so many ways, it's no wonder that people are so likely to use food to celebrate and soothe, that they hold the activity of eating in such high regard, that, indeed, life is planned around and toward eating.

Then there's the influence of American culture. Food ads and commercials, fast-food and fine restaurants, and supermarkets in the United States all shout that bigger is better when it comes to eating and getting your money's worth. Jumbo-sized bags of food, 16-ounce steaks, double and triple cheeseburgers, "all-you-can-eat" buffets—all exemplify the ever-present urgings of American society to eat more. Put it together with what you've learned from your family heritage, and don't be surprised that you have some eating habits that are tough to alter. Tough, yes, but not insurmountable when you're armed with the knowledge of how you got where you are and how to get to a new place. Read on to start a new way of thinking and eating.

Tip Sheet

Rewrite Your Family Food History

The influence of your family, your childhood, and your heritage on the way you eat can be complicated and far-reaching. You don't have to understand it all to change resulting eating behavior, but it is good to know the key ways in which you have been affected. It is also good to know that in most cases no one is to blame. Most likely your parents' understanding of eating issues and their knowledge of parenting options were limited. (More of this kind of information is accessible today.) Unless there was serious abuse involved, you can believe that they probably tried to do the best they could for you, and still do.

Every child is unique. She takes what she sees, learns, and understands from family dynamics and absorbs it in her own way. That is why Linda and her sister, while exposed to the same family, heritage, and food rituals, became very different in terms of the way they relate to food.

A person who overeats for emotional reasons needs to know that food is not love. It is not her parent; it is not her sole source of nurturance. But she can and should take pleasure in food and use it to nurture her body. Here are ways to begin changing problem-eating behaviors that relate to your family and culture.

❶ "Bio" Feedback

Write a short biography of your mother, father, sister or brother if you have one, and yourself. These need be only a paragraph or two pointing out the main qualities that make each person tick, including his or her food attitudes and behaviors (good and not so good). For example, a mother may be warm, caring, smart, and passionate, though she does not take good care of herself. She eats whenever she is bored and tends to eat a lot of junk food. She seems to be more concerned and critical about her family's habits than she is about her own. She is loyal and protective.

After you have written these "bios," circle the qualities in each that you think are desirable and underline the less-desirable ones. Notice the points that you have in common with your family members and the points where you differ. Make a conscious effort to play up the good points in yourself and perhaps emulate the qualities you admire in the others. Make a conscious decision to reject the issues in yours and the other bios that you feel are unappealing or self-defeating. Finally, list all the desirable traits in all the bios on one sheet of paper and read the list several times a day.

❷ It's Better in a Letter

Write a letter to your parents—without mailing it—explaining that there are things about the way they eat and the way you learned to eat from them that don't work for you. Tell them about your frustrations with eating and why you want to change your behavior. Explain briefly the family food attitudes that are a problem for you. Tell them you are working to break the old habits that have led you to problem eating. Let them know that all of this is separate from the rest of your relationship with them. Tell them you do not blame them for your problems but that you can no longer eat the way they do.

You are writing this letter for yourself, to clarify in your own mind the role that your parents had in shaping your eating behavior. Now, however, you are taking responsibility for your own behavior and, in a sense, divorcing yourself from your family's eating habits. You are doing this to take charge of your life, to make yourself happy, to feel good about yourself. You are not trying to change anyone but yourself here; hence, there is no reason to actually mail the letter.

③ Get Trigger-Ready

Think about any encounters with family members that can push your eating buttons on a regular basis. Do phone conversations with a sibling send you straight for the refrigerator? Do you tend to overeat when you go out to lunch with your mom? Do you and your dad sit in front of the TV and munch when he comes to visit? Prepare for these trigger situations ahead of time with a concrete plan of action.

For example, tell yourself that after any phone chat with a relative, you will immediately go outside for a few minutes and take several long, deep breaths of fresh air. The deep breathing will calm you and quell the urge to eat when you are not really hungry. Make this practice a habit that will replace the old, undesirable habit of eating to calm yourself in these situations. For eating-out family issues, think about what you'll order before you go—and stick to it. Include a small treat, like a bowl of sorbet, if you know you'll want a sweet. Make this your regular out-to-lunch-with-mom meal, and watch that old pattern disappear. For Dad and TV, switch to doing something with your hands, like playing cards and sipping iced tea. Again, plan ahead and know that this is what you're going to do.

④ Rethink Family Get-Togethers

Visiting the old homestead can bring back all sorts of memories—and behaviors. Here again, a little preplanning can work wonders.

▶ Bring your own breakfast. To make sure you start each day right, don't let bacon and eggs get the better of you if you're used to a plain bagel and fruit. Make sure you have your own staples on hand.

▶ Stay out of the kitchen. If the folks' refrigerator is a sure lure, just don't go in there if you can help it. Instead, bring your walking shoes or your tennis racket, get out of the house, and do something active.

▶ Don't get bored. See above.

▶ When you sit down to family meals, meditate silently for a moment. Think about eating slowly, enjoying the food, eating only until you are satisfied, and taking pleasure in the company of your loved ones.

▶ Escape when you need to. Don't let those family dramas push you to over-eat. Decide ahead that when you get riled up, you're going to STOP, collect yourself, and go out for a 10-minute brisk walk by yourself.

◆

Chapter 4

The Mind-Body Connection

"*Sometime between the ages of seven and nine, I gained a lot of weight," says Ila S., 38, a nurse who lives in southern California. "Mom said to me, 'You're getting kind of heavy,' and she put me on a diet. That made me different from most of the other kids in two ways. Not only was I heavy, but I had to be dieting too. It seems I was on one diet or another all through my childhood. I felt out of place. I was the kid in school most likely to be picked on. I was quiet and shy and didn't know how to fight back, I guess. All in all, I didn't feel very good about myself."*

For Ila it started in childhood. She was heavier than her peers and made to feel that was not acceptable. She was put on a diet at a young age, which made her feel even less acceptable. And so a pattern of low self-esteem began.

When you think about it, it's a pretty odd thing that for so many women, one's sense of self is ruled by the size and shape of one's body. It's not as if the body is the only thing a woman has going for her. People have intelligence, personality, warmth, humor, creativity, drive, energy, compassion, plus a great capacity to love and be loved. And this is only the shortlist of human attributes. So why is it, then, that when a woman feels "fat," she basically feels lousy about herself? And why is it that when something goes wrong in a woman's life, she feels fat?

There are two main concepts that enter into this picture. They are *body image* and *self-esteem.* Body image is the picture of the size and shape of your body that you see in your mind. It plays a large part in the way you see and feel about yourself as a whole—as well it should. After all, your body is the physical instrument you use to express yourself. It's only natural that you would want to take care of it, to keep it in good shape and working order. Self-esteem is your level of inner confidence and satisfaction based on your own judgment of yourself, not on the praise or judgment of others.

The problem lies in the fact that societal and cultural influences dictate how women should look and what size their body should be. The fashion and cosmetic industries set a standard that is constantly trumpeted by the media. And these days, although lobbying for the stick-thin image may be relaxing a bit, very trim is still very in. This is the standard, feminism or no feminism, by which many women judge themselves. Since it is impossible for all women to conform to this ideal image, many women's body images become distorted. That perfect model body out there leads women to believe that there is something wrong with their body—usually that it is too big or misshapen. The result often is that a woman can no longer see a clear picture of her body in her mind.

The other part of the problem is that society has placed far too great an emphasis on physical appearance. In other words, thinness is beauty, and beauty should be a dominant measure of worthiness. That's why many women's self-esteem is so tied to how they think their bodies look. Research shows that this body image/self-concept connection starts at a young age, as early as the fourth grade for girls (not so for boys). And it intensifies as girls get older.

Eventually a woman's focus on her body may become excessive. Her self-esteem may then enter a constant state of flux: if she feels thin or has lost a few pounds, her sense of self is strong; if she falls off her diet or has a bad day in general, she feels fat and worthless.

What does all this have to do with overeating? Plenty.

Guilt, Shame, and Self-Blame

Anyone who's ever read a weight-loss book or been through a diet program has probably heard that she is not to blame for being overweight. Masses of research points to genetic, societal, and emotional reasons for weight gain—reasons that this book will help you understand and deal with. Even so, there have most likely been times, and there can be again, when you felt guilty for overeating, ashamed of weighing more than you think you should (that ideal image again), and convinced that it was all your fault. When the world at large tells you that you can control your weight with diet, exercise, and discipline, it's pretty hard not to feel ashamed.

What happened next? If you're like many women, the guilt or shame you experienced stimulated other feelings:

▶ Anger—at yourself for being weak or undisciplined, or at the world because it isn't fair that you have this problem.

▶ Self-hatred—you deserve to be fat because you're worthless.

▶ Hopelessness—no matter how much you try, nothing ever changes, so what's the use.

▶ Depression—stemming from an inability to manage the feelings that result from the guilt and shame of overeating.

In order to cope, you may have used food to soothe yourself. You temporarily felt better through the comfort that food as nurturance provided. But later you may have felt guilty and ashamed all over again for giving in to the need to eat for comfort and contributing to your weight issues. And so the cycle goes.

There's another layer to this scenario. Have you ever said to yourself, "As soon as I lose 10 pounds, I'll take a vacation (or look for a new job, or buy a new dress, or . . . you get the idea)?" A women who feels bad about herself because she isn't at the weight she thinks she should be can easily get into the habit of postponing pleasure. Her shame about the way she looks or the way she eats translates into a feeling of being undeserving. She shouldn't get the things she wants, do fun activities, or be rewarded in any way. She also may want to hide herself. Why would she want to be out there exposing herself when she doesn't like the way she looks? The result, unfortunately, is that she may cut herself off from enjoyable activities—activities that could serve to nurture her and encourage her to feel happy and good about herself.

There is, however, a method of self-nurturing that some women practice alone, in private, when their self-esteem is flagging. This, of course, is eating. This is one more way the habit of eating for comfort is reinforced.

The Diet Conundrum

"Until I joined Weight Watchers, I was on and off diets my whole life," says Ila. "I'd lose some weight and then I'd feel good about myself. Then I guess I'd get cocky and feel I didn't need to do this anymore, and then I'd gain the pounds back. I'd get upset with myself and go on a diet again. And on and on. I got so tired of feeling bad about myself."

If you're reading this book, chances are you've been on a diet. And chances are you've been on a diet that failed. If so, you can probably relate to certain bad feelings that come with the territory. Highly restrictive diets, those that make you feel continually deprived, are a setup for self-esteem busting. This may seem a contradiction in terms because a diet, you reason, is supposed to help you lose weight and feel better about yourself. But look at the research.

Some studies conclude that many who lose weight on a diet will gain the weight back. A majority of obesity experts suggest that the feelings of deprivation brought on by stringent diets provoke many to lose their resolve and overeat as a result. This is supported by a recent study at Case Western Reserve University in Cleveland, which shows that self-denial wears a person down, causing ego depletion leading to a weakening of willpower. Research out of Baylor College of Medicine in Houston reveals that subjects who experienced dieting weight fluctuations over the course of a year exhibited more signs of depression, stress, and low self-esteem than those who stayed a constant higher weight during the same period.

This suggests a case of "the cure may be worse than the disease," if you'll pardon the analogy. The feeling of low self-worth (and other negative emotions) that results from dieting difficulties is likely to fuel more bouts of overeating. Does this mean you should never again try to lose weight? That it's hopeless? Absolutely not.

Eating Away at Self-Esteem

For a person who feels bad about herself, food can be a powerful tool. She may use it for control because eating may seem the one thing in her life over which she feels she has any control. She may see it as a comforting friend when she feels unloved or unworthy of being loved.

Here are ways people use food to deal with self-esteem issues. If these behaviors touch a chord, pay attention to the information in this chapter.

▶ You overeat to avoid social contact. By keeping yourself looking and feeling unattractive, you hope to keep others away from you.

▶ You overeat to avoid sexual attention. By maintaining overweight, you feel you can ward off unwanted sexual advances.

▶ You see overeating and large binges as a way of punishing yourself. Why? You've tried to lose weight and failed. You are weak and deserve to feel bad about yourself.

▶ You overeat to punish someone else. Your husband, for instance, is distressed about your overeating and has let you know about it. He hurt you, so this is how you get back at him.

▶ You eat and/or binge alone. This "secret" behavior empowers you —you know something that no one else knows.

▶ You feel depressed most of the time about your inability to lose weight. Eating is the only thing that will numb the pain.

In fact, other studies point to successes experienced by those participating in weight-loss programs. For example, in 1993 Weight Watchers International commissioned a study to find out how lifetime members (a qualification based on achievement of a reasonable goal weight and at least six weeks' maintenance of that weight within two pounds) were doing. The results showed that 67 percent of lifetime members overall, and 37 percent who'd been lifetime members for five years or more, had maintained their weight within five pounds. This is a far cry from the perhaps mythic 95 percent regain rate statistic that has circulated in the media in recent years.

A recent overview study at Temple University shows that weight control is worth the effort, that an effective program of weight management should combine *moderate* changes in food intake and activity along with an understanding of what it means to be at a *reasonable* weight for your body type. Easier said than done? Perhaps. But one thing is certain: when you put your body-image and self-esteem issues into proper perspective, you have a much better shot at putting your body in the shape you want it to be in. This chapter can help you to achieve this.

Why It's Tough to Keep Your Spirits Up

There's no question about how tricky it is to feel good about yourself these days. Although you have reasons to feel proud and happy, at times the world doesn't seem to support maintaining a positive stance. If you're overweight, you may get even less support. In fact, overweight is a condition that may be the most stigmatized by society. Examples of negative inferences about overweight people include:

They are to blame for their condition.

They are not attractive.

They are lazy.

They are undisciplined.

They are less intelligent than slim people.

In fact, none of these inferences are any more true for overweight people than for nonoverweight people.

There is evidence, however, that being overweight has negative economic and social effects. For instance, it's not uncommon for overweight people to face job discrimination, with the result that they settle for lower pay than their skills and experience warrant. Another example: Comedians have for years made jokes about fat people and still do.

The outcome of this social stigmatization: again, a poor sense of body image and lowered self-esteem. Even women who are only slightly over their "ideal" weight feel stigmatized. They keep hearing and reading messages from every imaginable source that there is something wrong with them if they are not thin. The issue in this case is that women tend to blame themselves for these negative social consequences rather attributing them to society or the attitudes of others. Again, compulsive overeating or bingeing may be used to escape from this negative self-related feeling.

That's why self-worth has to come from inside and not outside. Remember the definition of self-esteem stated at the beginning of this chapter? It should be based on your own judgment, not the judgment of others. It needs to evolve from a more realistic, self-embracing sense of body image that is not dictated by the pages of a fashion magazine.

Separating Self-Love, Body Issues, and Food

"All of my life people said I was a good listener," reveals Ila. "I cared about other people. But I didn't feel like I knew how to take care of myself or change how I felt about myself. The difference in my self-esteem—and my efforts to lose weight—came in 1994, when I joined Weight Watchers. Besides finding out what healthy eating was about, I got a lot of support from others. People accepted me for who I was, whether or not I took off or gained weight. Through them I learned to accept myself for exactly who I am. I learned to attend to my own needs, that I need time just for myself. Now I do things for myself that make me feel good about myself, like getting my nails done twice a month or perking up my hair color. I go to movies or for a walk instead of eating a lot. It all helps me to keep feeling good about myself."

Ila learned that she could change her mind about how she felt about her body. In addition, she realized that accepting and appreciating her own worth didn't have to depend on how much she weighed. Yes, she made the choice to eat in a more healthy manner and lose weight. But this choice was made possible by her improved body image and self-acceptance. She realized that she could like herself whether or not she was at an "ideal" weight. This helped her believe that she deserved pleasure—that she should take time to do nice things for herself. For Ila part of being nice to herself was eating healthy and shedding and keeping off the weight that made her feel uncomfortable. And she did.

No question, it's tough to be a woman today and not base your self-esteem on your appearance. It's tough to nurture yourself in ways other than eating when eating is the way you are used to doing it. On the other side of the picture, it's also tough to continually feel bad about yourself,

Profile

Name: Cindy M.

Location: Delaware

Age: 35

Career: Weight Watchers Leader and receptionist

Lost: 25 pounds

One of Cindy's biggest triumphs in her weight-loss efforts has been learning to identify a "normal" portion. In the past, a serving of sweet cereal could have been two to three times as much as it should be.

Growing up, I always had a great fear of gaining weight. My father is 5'6" and has weighed as much as 230 pounds. His sister is around 275 pounds. Deep down, I always thought I could end up like that.

My family was big on rewarding anything we did with food. "Let's go out and have a treat" was the way we handled a celebration, and I grew up surrounded by large quantities of food. We ate large dinners and were all heavy snackers; big bags of potato chips were always nearby. And I loved sweet cereal as a snack.

I wasn't overweight as a child. My weight problem started after I got married. During the first 10 years of marriage, I gained 10 to 15 pounds. Then I got pregnant. A year after my son was born, I was still heavy. I was eating whatever I wanted. I had no time to prepare good fresh foods.

Deep down, I just didn't think I deserved to be on a diet. I didn't want to feel deprived. If I tried to diet, it never lasted long, so the weight just kept creeping up. I was in denial about gaining weight for the longest time. I didn't want to see how I looked, so I avoided looking.

I would eat while watching TV at night, whether or not I was hungry. If I read a book, I had a snack. When I was home raising my son, I wasn't active enough and got bored. I ate during the day, either snacking or eating an extra meal. Eating gave me something to do and made the time pass. It became a hobby.

What turned me around were the two pictures of me taken within a month of each other. I could no longer deny that I was heavy and had to lose weight. This was just not the image I had of myself.

I have a girlfriend who is extremely independent and intelligent. She lost 60 pounds on Weight Watchers and kept it off. I thought, if she could do it, why couldn't I? Within a month of seeing the pictures, I went to my first meeting.

At Weight Watchers I learned about portion sizes. I also learned about the need for support. In the past I hadn't had the self-discipline to get the weight off and keep it off alone, but now I had this connection to others who were dealing with what I was dealing with. I learned how others handled difficult moments with food and what they did about it. It was helpful to know I was not alone. The structure of going ev-

> *I was in denial about gaining weight for the longest time. I didn't want to see how I looked, so I avoided looking.*

ery week and developing new habits to replace old, bad ones really worked for me.

I've lost and kept off 25 pounds for $2^1/_2$ years. My weight loss bubbles over to other areas of my life as well. Now I feel much more confident, self-assured, and assertive—I am worth something.

◆ ◆ ◆

eat to make yourself feel better, feel bad about yourself for doing that, eat to soothe yourself again, and so on. The point is that learning a new way of thinking about yourself and behaving takes time and effort, but you've probably spent a lot of time feeling and behaving in ways that have left you feeling trapped. So the time to start reshaping your self-image is now.

First, take the pressure off yourself. It's not your fault that society prizes thinness and tells you that beauty and worthiness come in a trim, fit package. You know, logically, that people are genetically programmed to be in all shapes and sizes. Realize that your feelings about your own body are partly shaped by society's urging to conform to a rigid standard. If you are struggling with overeating and overweight, understand that your issues are at least as much the result of these outside attitudes as they are the result of your weight itself. This is not to say that society is wholly to blame for your battle with food. But neither are you to blame. It's not about blame.

Next, learn to live for today. This is about accepting yourself, with all of your assets and all of your flaws, as you are right now. If you feel shame for the way you look or guilt over eating behaviors, you need to forgive yourself. By now you've begun to understand some of the many factors that contribute to your eating and body issues. There are a lot of forces at work here, and they didn't manifest themselves in you because you are bad or weak. When you realize this, you can move past shame and guilt and begin to focus on ways to make yourself feel good on a daily basis. As you develop the habit of treating yourself well—pursuing pleasurable activities other than eating, being with friends, focusing on your health, enjoying small indulgences (a bubble bath, a juicy novel, a manicure)—you cannot help but feel better about yourself.

Next, realize that you like yourself. The more you nurture yourself, the more you will feel worthwhile. This is the beginning of your newly boosted self-esteem. It's kind of a self-fulfilling prophesy: "I treat myself well because I am worth it; I am worth it because I am a unique, valuable, worthy person." Then, to augment these feelings, focus on your skills, talents, and qualities. Assess what you're good at: the contribution you make to your workplace, your artistic abilities, what you offer to your family, your sensitivity, compassion, and other personal attributes. Don't forget the small things, those positives that you would appreciate in others but would downplay when evaluating yourself.

Finally, go after what you *really* want—not some idealized version of what you think you *should* want based on outside attitudes. It can be anything you truly desire for yourself. Appreciating your self-worth will allow you to pursue and achieve your dreams. Just try to remember each day that you like yourself. Go easy on yourself. Enjoy the moments. What this is all about is a more realistic view of your body, leading to increased self-acceptance, leading to improved self-esteem, leading to the energy and optimism needed to make the changes you want to make. Then you'll be ready to stop using food as a way to stuff bad feelings, as a way to punish yourself for guilt or shame, as a way to keep yourself isolated. Then you'll be ready to adopt an eating habit that will serve you and your body well.

Tip Sheet

The Care and Feeding of the Self

Just as feeling bad about yourself can lead to overeating, which leads to feeling bad about yourself and more overeating, so can taking care of yourself lead to self-acceptance, which leads to greater self-esteem, which leads to taking better care of yourself and fulfilling your needs. You don't need to lose weight to start the ball rolling. But you do need to start being good to yourself.

Start with one of the strategies offered here. Get it going. Then get another one off the ground. You'll see how one good thing will fuel the next as you feel better and better about yourself as a person.

❶ Polish Your Image

Psychologists agree that caring for your body can help you foster a steady sense of security about your image. One way to jump-start body appreciation and attention is to pick three of your physical attributes that you feel best about—for example, your mouth (including your smile), your legs, and your hair. Focus on one of these assets for each of the next three weeks, doing the most that you can to play it up and show it off.

If you choose your mouth for the first week, buy yourself a really good lipstick in a wonderful color (an indulgence that will cost $15, tops) and wear it often. Use a lip liner with your lipstick to accentuate the shape of your mouth. Take special care of your teeth, perhaps using a whitening toothpaste to brighten your smile. Apply moistening lip balm every night before you go to sleep.

The next week, continue to show off your mouth as you focus on your legs. Shave them or go for a waxing the first day. Apply moisturizing cream to your legs morning and night, taking the time to really massage them. Buy a silky new pair of panty hose. Wear a short skirt often. Do morning leg stretches to get the circulation going so your legs will feel great every day.

The third week, keep the momentum going as you focus on your hair. Go get a trim or, better yet, a whole new style and color if you wish. Brush your hair 100 strokes every night, just for the feel of it. Use gel or clips to try variations on your usual style. Get that new conditioner you've been thinking about trying.

Whatever body parts you select, be creative in how you pamper them. Have fun and make your special treatment of yourself a lasting habit that will eventually spill over to all parts of you.

❷ Support Yourself

As is the case with many overeaters, you may have a tendency to isolate yourself. When self-esteem is flagging, it seems easier to retreat than to reach out for others. But social support, especially from those who deal with the issues that you do, can be a very effective way to help you realize your worthiness (as was the case for Ila). People who are working toward or have had success in changing eating behaviors can share their experience, listen to you, help you be more objective about yourself, comfort you, guide you toward healthier behavior, and help you to love yourself for who you are inside. They are there with you, or they've been there, so they know how you are feeling and can help you work toward your goals. What's more, studies show that those who have social support are better able to keep weight off than those who don't.

Support can come in a variety of forms. It may be a few women in your aerobics class who decide to join forces to work on the common goal of healthy eating habits. You can discuss emotional issues, call one another to share feelings and lend encouragement, have meals together, food shop together, and monitor your progress. Support can also be a group organized by a therapist or an organized weight-loss program. Wherever you choose to find it, don't be afraid to take the plunge. It might seem hard at first, but give it a chance.

After a time, assess whether you feel comfortable with your support system and whether it is helping you achieve improved self-esteem and better eating behavior. If things aren't improving for you, look for other support options. Don't give up. The alternative—social isolation—is a sure detriment to your self-esteem.

❸ Indulge Yourself

A simple but effective way to tell yourself "I'm worth it" is to begin a routine of pleasurable activities, right now. You don't have to spend a lot of money or take a long vacation to do this. First, make a list of "small indulgences" (other than eating) that you know you would enjoy. Examples might be:

▶ getting a manicure

▶ having a massage

▶ going to a movie

▶ buying a new scarf

Then plan a reasonable schedule of these activities in your monthly calendar. For instance, you could pop in for a manicure once every two weeks. A half-hour massage one Saturday a month wouldn't hurt your budget at all. A little gift every Friday after work—why not flowers?—would be a nice reward for a job well done. Get the idea? Make these little pleasures a regular habit, and notice how feeling good about yourself becomes a habit as well. By establishing self-nurturing rituals such as these, you'll find you have less need to nurture yourself with excess food.

❹ Give It Away

A surefire way to feel better about yourself is to help others to feel better. Volunteer. Give some of your time, energy, and heart to a cause that can use your help. Choose a project that really interests you, one that will offer an outlet for some of your special gifts. For example, if you love animals, spend an afternoon each weekend helping at an animal shelter. If you feel you're good at comforting others, consider helping out at home for the aged or perhaps an AIDS hospice. Like building things? Become involved in a community housing project such as Habitat for Humanity.

Giving of yourself in this way can offer you multiple benefits. Studies show that volunteering increases participants' self-esteem, improves mood, and even bolsters general health. You'll spend less time focusing on food and your weight and more time thinking about others' well-being. You'll also isolate yourself less as you participate in the social interaction that is the very essence of volunteerism.

⑤ Your "Want" List

Part of bolstering self-esteem is going after the things you want. This isn't just about huge life goals, although they're a part of it. It's also about small desires and everyday needs that help to fulfill you. Start by making a list of all kinds of things you think you want, even those that seem impossible. Make the list as short or long as you want. Don't edit yourself.

An example of a "want list":

Make more money.

Have more time to relax.

Lose 25 pounds.

Win the lottery.

Tell off my sister.

Be four inches taller.

Quit my job.

Take a trip to Hawaii.

Eat normally.

Learn in-line skating.

Treat my husband nicer.

Assess your list. First, draw a line through any wants that are out of the realm of possibility, like being taller. Then note the wants that might have troublesome consequences, like telling off your sister or quitting your job. Perhaps these can be adjusted to become more possible. For instance, you could gently tell your sister one thing about her behavior toward you that makes you feel bad, or you could work toward finding a better job for yourself.

Now consider the wants that can really happen. Some will be easy for you to achieve if you let yourself, like taking more time to relax. Others will take more effort, like learning in-line skating or making a trip happen. Start by making the simpler ones a reality. Each achievement will generate good feelings about yourself that will help you go for the next. Realize that you can make them happen, that you deserve them, that with a little energy you will get them.

Chapter ⑤

Are Daily Ups and Downs Eating at You?

"*It always seems like, no matter how well I'm doing with the food thing, there are certain days or periods of days when I just can't control myself at all,*" *reveals Cheryl M., 33, an office manager from the Twin Cities area of Minnesota. "I walk around in a bad mood and just feel so jittery all the time. Everything my husband says or does will tick me off and I get really mad at him. The traffic on the street as I drive to work makes me furious. And I'll start crying at the littlest things, which isn't such a good thing at work, if you know what I mean. Of course, these are the times when I just can't stop eating. I just have to calm myself down because I can't stand how bad I feel. I realize that I have PMS, and that this is probably what's making me feel so nuts, but every time it creeps up on me, I don't do anything about it except eat more. Sometimes I feel this way for ten days in a row. That's a lot when you consider this happens to me pretty much every month. And let's not even talk about those insane chocolate cravings. I just have to have it."*

The urge to overeat isn't always the result of a major, ongoing issue such as poor self-esteem, anger, or intense anxiety. If you're in the habit of using food to manage feelings, you may also be using it to regulate your overall mood. For all the same reasons that food numbs larger feelings for you—it's comforting, it's your friend, it's a distraction—it also helps you stabilize yourself when you feel edgy, blue, cranky, or tired.

Everyone has mood swings. Everyone goes through ups and downs on a regular basis. It's natural and human. Both men and women experience monthly hormonal fluctuations that may affect the way they feel from day to day. For many women these hormonal shifts may be more extreme and, when combined with a variety of other factors, can cause more severe mood variations and also changes in the body. They may indicate such conditions as premenstrual syndrome (PMS) and seasonal affective disorder (SAD), both of which are associated with times of increased eating. PMS and SAD can be tough to deal with for anyone. If you're a woman in the habit of eating to manage feelings, these conditions can be very tricky indeed.

The hard part about dealing with mood fluctuations is that they often sneak up on you and catch you by surprise. It's one thing to get angry about something and feel the swell of emotion, or to experience heavy job stress, or to be alone and bored in the house. These conditions are pretty self-evident. You can usually tell they are happening when they are happening. But when, for example, hormonal shifts bring on a low-level case of the blues or crankiness, you may not know what's hit you until it's all over, if at all. Nonetheless, these conditions can cause an emotional eater to reach for the snacks. This kind of behavior may not even seem like overeating, but as you probably know, it adds up. Before you know it, you've gained unwanted weight and you're not even sure why.

This chapter will help you understand what happens when your mood makes you reach for food—from mood changes brought on by the hormonal fluctuations of your menstrual cycle to the lows brought on by sheer fatigue. When you understand these day-to-day shifts and are prepared for them, you will be ready to ward off the urges to overeat they can promote.

It's Not All in Your Head

A natural and constant part of your life as a woman is living from cycle to cycle. During the course of a 21- to 35-day time period (this is the normal range for most women), your body prepares itself to host an egg released from your ovary that may become fertilized through conception. If no fertilization occurs, the egg, plus the lining of your uterus, is shed through menstruation.

It takes a complicated series of hormonal changes to implement this process cycle after cycle. Various hormones, or chemical messengers, travel through the bloodstream to make things happen in various parts of your body. To understand how much your hormones fluctuate in a month or so, here is a brief description of their activity during your menstrual cycle.

Starting with the first day of your cycle, which is the first day of menstrual bleeding, your brain releases follicle stimulating hormone (FSH), which causes a few eggs in one of your ovaries to mature. As one egg develops further, surrounding cells form a casing called a follicle. At the same time the production of another hormone, called estrogen, increases in the body; the estrogen moves to the uterus, where it stimulates the tissue in the uterine lining to grow.

About halfway through your cycle, your estrogen and FSH levels peak, prompting a surge in luteinizing hormone (LH), which causes the ripe egg to be released from your ovary into the fallopian tube (ovulation). The remaining follicle matures into what's called a corpus luteum, which is responsible for the secretion of still another hormone, progesterone. Progesterone works to make the uterus ready to host the fertilized egg. If the egg is not fertilized, it is absorbed into your body. By day 26 or so of your cycle, your level of progesterone falls sharply along with a further decrease in estrogen. This prompts the lining of your uterus to be shed, and menstruation begins. The cycle is now ready to start all over again.

This normal ebb and flow of body chemicals does more than just prepare your uterus for pregnancy once a month. Other physical changes occur as well. Your temperature drops a bit before ovulation and rises just after. This higher temperature holds until menstruation, when it drops to its norm. Hormonelike substances called prostaglandins are produced before and at menstruation and may cause pain or cramping. But some changes that occur during the time between ovulation and menstruation are the ones that seem to plague many women most. They contribute to a condition called premenstrual syndrome (PMS).

Chances are you have experienced symptoms of PMS at some time—if not every month—during your life. Many women do. The variety of symptoms include:

Bloating

Breast swelling or tenderness

Food cravings (often for chocolate or other sweets)

Increased general hunger

Decreased tolerance for alcohol

Depression

Mood swings

Irritability

Backaches

Headaches

Fatigue

Although there has been a great deal of research on the subject, the exact cause of PMS is difficult to pinpoint. There are strong indications that excess estrogen, progesterone-level fluctuation, and prostaglandin production in the body during the second half of your cycle play a role. There is also some speculative research indicating that decreases in the levels of the brain chemicals serotonin, dopamine, and endorphins during this phase of the cycle may contribute to PMS's symptoms, but these studies are inconclusive.

If you struggle with food, you are probably most curious about the symptoms that affect your body and your eating behavior. First, there's the bloating. It is probable that since progesterone helps the kidneys regulate sodium and fluid retention, the rapid drop in progesterone a couple of days before menstruation may be responsible for bloating during this period. Why does fluid retention affect an overeater? Consider the results of *Psychology Today*'s 1997 Image Survey: more than 75 percent of women say that "a

Caffeine and Sugar and Mood

There's been a lot of research about caffeine and sugar and how they affect the body. Caffeine is a stimulant that affects the central nervous system and heart. When you ingest a caffeinated food or beverage, the chemical is absorbed rapidly and distributed throughout your body, making you feel energized and more alert. Its effect is swift. But some people are more susceptible to caffeine's power than others. Yes, you experience a boost from it. But you may also experience a subsequent withdrawal as it wears off, which produces symptoms such as headaches, irritability, and fatigue if not countered with more caffeine. For an overeater, feeling irritable or tired or cranky can easily lead to an eating episode.

Sugar is a simple carbohydrate that is absorbed quickly into your bloodstream in the form of glucose, causing a rise in blood sugar. This rise is countered by your body's release of insulin, which pushes glucose from the blood to the cells. Your blood sugar then drops, sometimes to a lower level than before you ingested the sugar. The latest body of research says that the human body is more than capable of dealing with these physical effects and that the once-believed "sugar rush" is a myth. However, many overeaters swear that sugar causes problems for them: cravings for more sugary foods, energy highs and subsequent lows, increased appetite in general.

Because of individual body chemistry, one person may be more susceptible to the effects of caffeine than another. And perhaps it's a person's psychology that makes her feel that sugar is a problem. Whatever the reasons, some people report feeling irritable, tired, or depressed as an aftereffect of even one cup of coffee or a piece of candy. If you're in a battle with food, these feelings are apt to send you straight to the refrigerator.

Research out of the University of South Alabama shows that some depressed people (perhaps 20 to 30 percent) who remove caffeine and sugar from their diets experience greater energy and improved mood. Others who have given up these substances report a more even mood and energy level all around. On the other hand, both caffeine and sugar have benefits that cannot be denied: coffee- and tea-drinking rituals are a satisfying part of our culture, and caffeine has been shown to improve mental performance and concentration. And who can argue with the occasional pleasure of eating a wonderful dessert?

As you get to know more about your eating triggers, you can assess how much of a problem caffeine and sugar are for you. Some who have successfully conquered overeating have given up one or both entirely. Others have modified their intake of these substances with great results. See the Tip Sheet at the end of this chapter for ways to accomplish this.

certain time in my menstrual cycle" causes negative feelings about the body. As discussed in Chapter Four, negative body image may lead to bouts of overeating. Research has also shown that a woman's metabolic rate increases during the days prior to menstruation, leading to increased hunger and caloric intake.

PMS is a very real condition that has a very real affect on the way you feel and your eating behavior. Many women deal with these symptoms every month. Why some women are affected more intensely than others is perhaps due to their individual body chemistry. It's vital, however, to understand that this is a very natural part of life. What you need to do is learn ways to deal with these conditions, which are also natural—and healthy. For some simple strategies, see the Tip Sheet at the end of this chapter.

Why Do You Think They Call It SAD?

"You know, up here in Minnesota we have very cold, very dark winters," says Cheryl. "You'd think I would have gotten used to them, but the fact is I don't do so well during this time of year. I get depressed a lot and I feel more tired that usual. But the worst thing is that I feel a lot hungrier. I just feel that I have to have really big meals with a lot of starches in order to feel better. I always gain a lot of weight in the winter and then I fight all spring and summer to get it off. Boy, am I tired of that!"

Have you noticed that, like Cheryl, you tend to eat more and feel lethargic, even depressed, during the autumn and winter months? Whether you experience a mild case of this phenomenon, sometimes referred to as "winter blues," or the more extreme symptoms that suggest seasonal affective disorder (SAD), the struggle with escalated urges to eat can be frustrating.

Many people experience winter blues. The period of cooler weather combined with less daylight promotes a decrease in activity and exercise. The result is diminished energy and increased fatigue—two conditions that may lead to eating more.

SAD is less prevalent but far more debilitating. What causes it? Research suggests that decreased exposure to light is the culprit. When light hits the retina of the eye, it causes a brain function that decreases the production of the sleep-inducing, hormonelike chemical melatonin in the body. In cooler months, when daylight is shortened and the weather causes overcast skies, people are exposed to less light and are subject to higher melatonin levels.

In addition, serotonin levels drop as melatonin levels increase, because serotonin is actually converted to melatonin in the brain. As discussed previously, serotonin may regulate mood, and low levels could result in a variety of symptoms, including food cravings. Studies also indicate that dopamine levels decrease when light exposure is reduced. Since this nerve chemical affects alertness, lower levels may promote the drowsiness and inability to concentrate associated with SAD.

As many as one in ten people are afflicted with SAD. Many more women than men suffer from it; researchers are not sure why this is so. Symptoms, which are similar to those of PMS, include:

Food cravings

Increased hunger

Marked weight gain

Lethargy and fatigue

Anxiety

Depression

Heightened sensitivity to pain

Intensified PMS symptoms

Since SAD can plague sufferers three to four months out of every year, its affect on mood, appetite, and weight can be significant, if not heartbreaking. But SAD does not mean hopeless. If you know or suspect that you have SAD, consider light therapy. Studies show that exposure to intense, full-spectrum light (which mimics the light of early morning) for one or two hours a day or less helps to reduce appetite and cravings and elevate mood for many people with the disorder.

Once again, knowledge is power. Being aware that winter blues or SAD may be affecting your daily attitude and the way you eat can set you on a course to combat adverse conditions.

Are You Hungry—or Tired?

Fatigue has all kinds of consequences. Feelings of stress intensify. Little irritations seem like big problems. Your patience can quickly wear thin, and this can affect relationships with family members and co-workers. You have less energy, so you may be less likely to participate in physical activity, one thing that can give you more energy. Fatigue may cause a good mood to plummet. Fatigue may also spur you to eat.

The logical thing to do when you feel tired is to sleep. But the overeater is not always logical, nor can you just lie down and take a nap anytime you feel like it. Perhaps it goes back to Mom saying, "Eat, you'll feel better." Or perhaps you feel that food perks you up and gives you energy. Whatever the underlying motivation, many people who have issues with food report that they overeat when they are tired. Often they reach for sweets to give them that temporary lift.

The problem is that eating is not the answer here. When you are tired, it's probably because you need rest, not food. Unfortunately, sleep deprivation is all too common in this fast-paced society. About 70 percent of all adults say that they regularly do not get enough sleep. If you are prone to eating as a result of fatigue, you owe it to yourself to find ways to get more sleep. Get into the habit of going to sleep earlier at night. Studies show that going to bed and waking up earlier on a regular basis help improve the quality of sleep. Try to nap if you can. A mere 20 minutes can revitalize you. When you feel drained and you're about to reach for food, ask yourself first if you are tired. If you are, you need to deal with that issue appropriately, which means get more sleep, not eat more food.

It's the Little Things

"Sensitive? WHAT DO YOU MEAN I'M SENSITIVE?!" For many who struggle with food, or with any other substance, for that matter, little deals can often seem like big deals. Perhaps the constant tug-of-war with overeating, undereating, dieting, and weight control takes its toll on a person's objectivity and sense of perspective.

This is by no means to say that you don't know a big issue from a small one or that you overreact to everything. But many overeaters admit to being highly touchy and emotional about things. Says one: "I feel things deeply. Everything. Big things like a death in the family, to little things like a minor criticism from my boss. I did when I was eating, and I do now, even though I have conquered my battles with food. The difference is that now I let myself feel the feelings and try to deal with them without food."

The point is that a mood change often results from a little issue. And your mood can change a number of times in a day. Sometimes these small mood swings make you feel like munching. You're a little cranky—you eat. You're a bit ticked off at your husband—you eat. You're nervous about making a phone call at work—you eat. These aren't big deals, but they can promote the kind of emotional eating that brings on a creeping weight gain.

Eating to deal with moods and emotions—no matter what their cause—is an insidious habit that is supported by lots of repetition, but the habit can be broken with knowledge, understanding, and the practice of alternative behaviors. Assessing and then managing your day-to-day mood swings without food may seem like a tricky proposition. Moods creep up on you; they're often so subtle that you can't put your finger on them. The strategy, then, is to catch yourself reaching for the food and then say to yourself, "Stop. Is this about hunger, or is it about irritation, agitation, fatigue, or general moodiness?" If you build *this* habit into your lifestyle, you'll have a much easier time choosing other ways to handle your feelings besides eating.

Tip Sheet

Mood Soothing

Once you are aware of what sets off your mood fluctuations and how these little peaks and valleys affect your eating, you can make the choice to deal with them productively. Part of your mental preparation is to understand that there is a healthy and often simple way to react to these feelings. The hard part is turning yourself in this new direction instead of taking the "easy" way out with food. Eating does seem like an easy solution at the time, but living through the consequences of overeating—weight gain, guilt, and self-loathing—is anything but easy.

Although this book is not specifically about food choices, sometimes eating a certain way is the perfect solution for dealing with an emotional-eating issue. That's why there are strategies here that are designed to help you rethink the way you eat in response to cravings, the way certain foods affect you, and the way you eat your meals.

❶ Controlling Constant Cravings

To manage the intense cravings that set you off on a binge:

▶ Eat a little bit of something you love. Experts say that depriving yourself of a desired food, making it "forbidden," may be fuel for a future binge. But a controlled amount of that food may be just the trick to appease the overpowering craving. If, for instance, PMS makes you crave chocolate, be ready with one piece of the best chocolate. Eat it slowly, taste it, savor it. Tell yourself that chocolate is a normal food that will satisfy you in small amounts. A whole bag of store-bought chocolate-chip cookies won't work as well.

▶ Make the most of your meals, mood-wise. The key is to make meals as wonderfully satisfying as you can. Eat beautiful, fresh, very tasty foods that are particularly enjoyable to you. Sit down at a lovely place setting, or choose a lunch spot that is aesthetically desirable to you. When meals are a pleasurable experience, when the foods are wonderful, you'll be satisfied with less. You'll also be less prone to cravings and be less apt to snack on junk food between meals.

▶ Don't get too hungry. Make sure to eat meals at regular times when you're feeling emotionally edgy. If you skip meals or become overly hungry, you're more likely to eat a huge amount of food.

❷ Caffeine and Sugar Solutions

Coffee, soft drinks, tea, candy, cookies, and pastries are all part of this country's food culture. As a result, you're constantly exposed to them. For physical and perhaps psychological reasons, some people are more susceptible to issues with caffeine and sugar, while others aren't affected at all.

If you find yourself continually craving sweets or turning to caffeine for a lift, consider modifying your intake. One or two cups of a caffeinated beverage before midafternoon shouldn't cause much trouble. If you're drinking more, gradually cut down by drinking coffee that is half decaf or leaving the tea bag in for half the time you usually do. Opt for mineral water or seltzer over colas.

When sugar "calls" to you, reach for nutritious alternatives to empty-calorie sweets, such as high-fiber fruits like apples and oranges or whole-grain snacks. If you want sweets, have them after meals, when the food in your stomach will keep you from eating too much of them.

❸ Prepare for PMS

Beyond the mood swings that propel you to munch premenstrually, hormone and brain-chemical fluctuations may actually make you hungrier than otherwise. If PMS gets you down:

▶ Eat smaller meals more often to curb hunger and keep blood sugar steady throughout the day.

▶ Reduce your intake of caffeine, sugar, and alcohol, which may aggravate tension and irritability in some people.

▶ Drink a lot of water, which will help flush excess sodium (and bloat) from your system.

▶ Don't forget to engage in physical activity. Exercise calms you and curbs hunger and may help stabilize hormones and pump up feel-good endorphins. (Always consult your primary-care physician before beginning any new exercise regime.)

❹ Into the Light

If you're one who gets moody with the change in seasons, one of the best things you can do to ward off the symptoms of winter blues is to turn on the lights—literally. On dreary days and dark mornings, expose yourself to a steady stream of incandescent light (office-type fluorescent lighting is not effective). Increased light may raise your serotonin level and thereby improve mood and decrease winter appetite.

Turn on overhead and lamp lights as soon as you get up. If your work environment has fluorescent lighting, ask for a small incandescent table lamp for your desk, or bring your own. Bundle up and get out in the winter sunlight as much as possible.

Because even moderate exercise can help improve mood, a brisk lunchtime walk in the sunlight offers a double dose of treatment. Most of the above strategies for PMS can also help.

If your winter symptoms are severe and you suspect you may have SAD, see a physician for an accurate diagnosis and appropriate therapy. There are specially designed light boxes that can offer the right spectrum and intensity of light to ward off the effects of SAD.

Chapter 6

Stressed Out and Snacking

"*I've been on the heavy side my entire life, but I've really put on the pounds since I've been in the workplace,*" *admits Lynne S., a 32-year-old commercial sales manager for a large corporation in Chicago.* "*I can't tell you how many times I've been on the road, gone back to my hotel after a business meeting, and calmed myself with food. Being in sales is very stressful. In the beginning I had to make a lot of cold calls and break into a new market. I wasn't all that confident about myself, and that added to the stress of the work itself. The stress was like an immediate trigger for me. I'd feel anxious, and then I'd eat quickly and mindlessly to settle myself down. I just didn't know anything else that could comfort me the way food did.*"

You know about stress. Everyone does. You may notice it creep up on you or attack in a sudden burst. At times it's like a ripple through your body; at other times it may feel as though your whole system is in an ever-tightening vice. But when you feel it, you know it's stress. Even so, stress is difficult to define because it presents itself in so many different ways.

In the 1930s, pioneer researcher Hans Selye defined stress as the body's response to certain demands. The generally accepted theory today is that when an occurrence threatens a person's sense of freedom or control, she will experience physiological and psychological stress. Each person's unique perception colors the way she reacts to a potential stressor (cause of stress). That's why an event such as marriage will be intensely stressful to one person while much less so to another.

Stress results from external forces, such as the pressures of your job, a strain in your relationship, the lack of time to get everything done, or problems with your kids; it also stems from internal forces, such as negative thinking based on low self-worth or an unrealistic quest for perfection.

Some experts theorize that all stressors are either good, such as a falling in love, or bad, such as a marital breakup. Some mild forms of stress, such as that provoked by exercise, are beneficial and can result in improved performance and motivation. Any kind of stress causes a kind of arousal, the nature of which may feel positive or negative. While some researchers feel there are those who thrive on stress, others contend there's no real evidence to support this idea.

If there is one thing upon which researchers and therapists agree, however, it is that many people eat in reaction to stress and its resulting anxiety. People who are highly focused on food and weight may regularly use food as a calming mechanism. In addition, some studies, including one out of the University of Michigan at Dearborn that looked at gender variables in eating behavior after subjects watched an anxiety-provoking film, suggest that women may have a tougher time with stress eating than men. It's no surprise, then, that women often report that they gain weight during particularly stressful periods in their lives.

Like stress itself, this information may seem daunting. But have faith. There are very effective techniques for dealing with stress eating, even when your stress is vague and the source is difficult to determine. As you read the rest of this chapter, you'll gain an understanding of what stress is and how it affects your body and your mind. You'll then be able to determine your particular stressors, how you react to them, and which of the strategies offered here can help you the most.

Fight or Flight—or Feed

One thing about stress does seem to be constant—the body's "emergency reaction," or "fight-or-flight" response to it. Just as it happened to cave dwellers in the early days of human life, when someone perceives a stressor as a threat, her glands release hormones (including adrenaline) that cause her senses to sharpen, her heartbeat to quicken, and her blood pressure and blood sugar to elevate, all to ready her body to fight or flee the threat.

But here's the catch: Early humans did indeed use these stress-heightened capabilities to deal with physical danger—a hungry wild animal, a fierce storm. Today, however, a person is most often reacting to stressors that do not warrant an active, physical response—criticism from the boss, long lines at the supermarket, a near-miss collision in heavy traffic.

The accompanying pumped-up blood pressure and blood sugar and heightened emotions are not expended through running or fighting. Instead, the "juices" are left to simmer in the body and may evolve into intense feelings of agitation and anxiety.

If you're like many people, one way you quickly relieve anxiety is to eat. Whether you learned as a child that eating makes you feel better or discovered as an adult that food works like a mild tranquilizer, the habit of eating to calm yourself is enforced time after time because it does bring a kind of relief. But the relief is not only temporary but also problematic. As you most likely know, this form of relief may lead to overeating and weight gain, stressors in their own right.

What Exactly Is Anxiety?

If stress is the way you respond to certain demands that you perceive as a threat, anxiety is an emotional consequence of the stress. It is that vague but often powerful feeling of apprehension about something that may happen in the future, whether or not that something is a specific event. This feeling may cause you to become agitated or nervous. You may worry, obsess, experience a sense of panic, or even develop a phobia about a situation or object. In addition, you may experience physical reactions beyond those already described as part of the fight-or-flight response, including muscle tension (especially in the back and neck), uneven or shortness of breath, cold hands and feet, knots in the stomach, weak knees or legs, trembling, and sweating. (If you experience chronic anxiety that you are unable to cope with, consider seeking professional help.)

When anxiety is caused by a specific stressor, there's a good chance it can be addressed appropriately. For example, if you are anxious about presenting at an important meeting at work tomorrow afternoon, it is likely you will deal with the anxiety by making sure you are prepared for your role in the meeting.

If, however, you have a difficult time pinpointing the source of anxiety, you may be more likely to fall into habitual behaviors that offer you temporary relief, such as eating. One example of this kind of stress is the chronic pressure of facing too many demands, including working full time, raising kids, running a household, nurturing a marriage, and caring for aging parents. Remember that part of stress is the way you perceive obstacles. If you have unrealistic expectations about how well you should be accomplishing all of these tasks, your anxiety may be exacerbated.

This kind of ongoing stress may insinuate itself into your life to such a degree that it seems like a normal bodily function, like your heartbeat or breathing. The resulting feelings take on a free-floating quality, as if they were built in to your system. But that doesn't necessarily mean there's no tension. Eating may present itself as the perfect stress-management solution—you can do it anytime, food is always accessible, and it has quick results. Unfortunately, the solution is likely to become part of the problem, that is, when the stress of overeating causes further anxiety.

Women and Stress

It would be hard to deny that stress is inherent in women's lives today. Today nearly 75 percent of American women work outside the home. They are responsible for part, if not all (the ranks of single moms are growing), of their family's income and, at the same time, are the primary caretakers for their children and home. As they juggle these multiple roles

Exercise: Good Stress to Reduce Stress

If you were a Buddhist monk living in solitude in the mountains of Tibet, information on the benefits of exercise may not have reached your domain. But because you are a savvy person concerned about health and well-being, you've probably been exposed to countless books, articles, essays, news stories, and word-of-mouth accounts about how and why exercise can help you feel better physically and mentally. Exercise is such a universal tonic that it could be a strategy for dealing with nearly every issue in this book—and it will be mentioned more than a few times.

So why does it get a whole section in the text of this particular chapter? Because the research is conclusive, and most experts in the fields of obesity, psychology, stress management, and exercise physiology agree, that physical activity is one of the best ways to alleviate stress and anxiety. And many, including exercisers themselves, believe that the lasting effects include positive feelings of confidence and well-being that, along with the stress relief, help people overcome overeating and overweight.

"Part of what I do to deal with stress these days is regular morning runs along the lakeshore," says Lynne, who lives near Lake Michigan. "It helps me start my day relaxed and feeling strong. Plus, I get to take in the beauty of the natural surroundings as I run. I need visual stimulation, and this is one of the ways I can give that to myself while doing something else positive."

Interestingly, exercise is itself a stressor. It places the same kind of emergency-response demands on your body that other stressors do. But in this case the elevated heart rate and blood pressure work in tandem with the ongoing physical activity. At the same time the pent-up tensions and energy caused by other stressors are released. This means that while the exercise is strengthening your muscles, burning calories, boosting your metabolism, and providing cardiovascular benefits, it is also helping you to relax. If agitation and anxiety trigger your eating, relaxation is certainly one way to quell it.

There are other explanations for exercise's stress-reducing qualities:

▶ Researchers have shown that sustained exercise increases the brain's emission of alpha waves, an occurrence that also results from meditation. These brain waves are associated with a more relaxed mental state.

▶ Some believe that vigorous exercise sets off the body's release of endorphins, hormonelike chemicals that are known to promote feelings of calm and euphoria that can counter stress.

▶ Focusing on exercise provides distraction from negative thoughts and feelings and thereby a break from nagging stress.

With all of this in mind, remember that any kind of physical activity is a terrific alternative to emotional eating and the stress it causes you. (Consult your primary-care physician when entering into any new exercise program.) When you're about to grab a bag of chips or cookies, grab your workout shoes instead. At the office? Grab your coat and get yourself outside for a brisk walk.

and the resulting time pressures, they also contend with issues of financial security, unequal pay and job opportunity, the unrealistic but compelling need to do it all "perfectly," maintaining or finding a satisfying relationship, and more. All of these elements can induce stress in women. Add the pressures that come from overeating and overweight and the resulting esteem issues to the mix, and you have a potent stress cocktail.

Lynne understands this all too well. "In sales there's not a lot of control. Since I was also out of control with food, there wasn't much about my life that I felt control over. The relationship side of things also made me eat. I wanted a partner in life, but I was heavy, which I felt limited my options. I just didn't want to settle. The whole dating thing was stressful for me. The work was stressful; my body image made me uncomfortable. And I just kept eating."

Remember that stress is a reaction to a condition that disturbs your sense of freedom or control. When you think about the issues that women face today and the way that they have escalated in the past few decades, it's not surprising that women report being highly stressed more often than men do. Consider these examples of everyday stressors to help you understand what you're dealing with and how the issues affect you:

▶ Work—failure leading to loss of income; striving for better pay; intense competition; too many hours; too much responsibility.

▶ Home and family—not enough time for your children; your children's issues (health, school, relationships); housework burdens; care of aging parents.

▶ Relationship—keeping a marriage on track; finding a life partner; not enough nurturing friendships; a new relationship; relationship breakup; being alone.

▶ Feelings and perceptions—not being a good-enough mom; not being a good-enough partner; too fat; "faking it" at work; not smart enough to get a job.

Circumstances such as these create a baseline of stress for women. Although these issues seem intrinsic to life, they *can* be addressed, and their negative consequences can be improved. The following points may seem cliché; you may have read these ideas in countless women's magazines. Nonetheless, they bear repeating because they work. Here are four strategies that can really help to alleviate some of your chronic stress, stress that may contribute to overeating:

1. *Organization*—including setting goals, making lists, and making your home and/or office more efficient.

2. *Time management*—including prioritizing your responsibilities, making a reasonable schedule and doing your best to stick to it, and carving out nurturing alone-time for yourself.

3. *Delegation*—including giving employees, partner, and kids things to do that you usually do, sending out the laundry if you need to, ordering out for dinner, and then giving up control of the things you have delegated.

4. *Realistic thinking*—including knowing that you don't have to be perfect (as a mother, housekeeper, worker, or spouse) and accepting that you are doing your best.

Try focusing on the particular stressors that affect your life, one at a time. If, say, your time crunch is a constant source of agitation, stop and look at a typical day. Determine which responsibilities are a must and which can be postponed or even eliminated from your life.

Get a day-to-day planner and delegate blocks of time for each task you need to accomplish. Research shows that the simple act of writing out a list of tasks—and checking them off as you complete them—can in itself help ease stress. Then try to stick to your plan. Do the best you can, and don't sweat it if you can't follow the timeline exactly. Be creative about solving other issues. Many fine books on organization and time management are available to help you.

Nurturing a Stress-Weakened Body

It would be remiss to discuss how stress affects you and your eating without mentioning its affect on the immune system. No doubt you've heard that chronic stress can cause health problems. This is more than just a theory. According to the American Academy of Family Physicians, 50 to 60 percent of all illnesses are related to stress. The physical stress response, which includes elevated heart rate and blood sugar, seems to suppress aspects of the immune system, such as the effectiveness of disease-fighting white blood cells.

Stress may also be the culprit when it comes to low-level but often chronic maladies like fatigue, mild depression, allergies, and digestive problems. For those who eat to soothe themselves, the problem here is all too apparent. Besides using food to calm yourself from the stress of the moment, you may also use it as a form of nurturance when stress attacks your physical health. For one thing, as discussed in Chapter Five, fatigue is a primary trigger for many compulsive eaters. And fatigue is one of the first symptoms of a stress-weakened immune system. If food is your

Profile

Name: Jermel I.

Location: New York

Age: 27

Career: Quality analyst

Lost: 90 pounds

◆ ◆ ◆

Instead of keeping her feelings inside and turning to food for comfort, Jermel now insists on airing her emotions, either by writing in her journal or talking it out.

I was always overweight. I remember overeating as far back as elementary school—going to birthday parties and eating three hot dogs while the other kids ate one. My mom was very abusive. Between the physical and the emotional, it was just too much. So when I was sad, I'd eat a lot; that was how I coped. In school my sister and I were both A students. My mom praised my sister's work but never praised mine. That hurt me a lot. I overate, and sometimes it made me feel better, but usually it just made me feel miserable and really guilty.

In high school I worked in fast-food restaurants, and I ate. I never really saw myself as being overweight. It was normal for me—it was all I knew. But when I look back I see that I was much bigger than my friends. The only thing I hated was when people would say, "Oh, she's so beautiful, if only she wasn't so fat." I would cry sometimes. I think I wanted to lose weight, but I never really tried. I just accepted it as my life.

After I gave birth to my daughter about four years ago, I was 286 pounds. I really felt ugly. At that point it was like, "Okay, pretty soon I won't be able to wear plus sizes." I had reached a point where I wasn't happy. I was so tired—I couldn't walk up the stairs.

I decided I was going to be more positive and change things about myself. One day a woman from my church asked me how I felt. I told her I wasn't happy and I was very insecure about my weight. She told me to study the Bible and maybe something would hit me.

After a while something did hit me: I thought my weight really showed how out of control my life was. That's what motivated me to make the changes, and with the help of the Weight Watchers Program, I was really able to lose weight and be consistent about it. I would get up in the morning and go walking. I also liked how what I was doing encouraged other people to try to lose weight.

Before, I never talked about things. I would cry and go off by myself. Now I talk about how I'm feeling—even when I feel good. I realize now it's not eating that makes me happy. I love a good meal, but my heart doesn't feel

the same way about eating and food. I see how I used it in a destructive way, how I used it for comfort. If something hurt me, I used it to fulfill my needs. Food was like a drug for me.

I learned that I was someone who really sought comfort from the outside, that there was nothing within me that

"I hated when people would say, 'Oh, she's so beautiful, if only she wasn't so fat.'"

gave me comfort. I was really unhappy with who I was. I didn't get any comfort growing up, no nurturing. It's hard to look back on your life and see all that pain.

Now my mom and I are very close. I've spoken to her about how I felt growing up. She always thought I was someone who had confidence, but I told her I didn't. It took a lot of work.

I also had an aunt who called my sister Skinny Minnie and me Fatty Watty. This year I confronted her about it. Even though I'd lost 90 pounds, she was still saying, "What's up, Fatty?" I told her, "You know, that's really not encouraging. It's not helping me in any way. I've accomplished a lot and I would appreciate it if you wouldn't say that." She apologized. She said she didn't know it bothered me.

One positive force in my life is my husband. He has always supported me. He never once said "You need to lose weight." In fact, I think he was in denial. He recently saw an old picture of me and he was like, "Oh my gosh!" He fell in love with me and married me just the way I was. That has always been comforting for me. Now he encourages me and he's very proud of me. I get a lot of comfort from the fact that I'm in control and able to raise my daughter without imitating the patterns that were set up for me. Being able to break the cycle is encouraging. Having a way out, having examples that I can follow—that helps me and gives me great confidence.

habitual source of comfort, there's a good chance you reach for the pota-toes, the macaroni and cheese, or the chocolate when you're tired, sapped of energy, or suffering from other stress-induced ailments.

Because stress has immediate consequences (anxiety and/or other emotions) as well as delayed ones (health issues), its effect on your life can be doubly troubling. This is especially true if eating is your usual coping mechanism. It is crucial, then, that you learn alternative meth-ods for managing stress. This chapter offers a variety of sensible stress-busting techniques that can serve as alternatives to your stress-eating habit.

Eating as the Answer to Stress

Stress eating is a funny thing. You probably have a friend who just stops eating when stressed out. That probably annoys you because you head straight for the proverbial cookie jar whenever anxious feelings hit. To you, eating may seem a totally natural reaction to stress. In fact, it's not.

When that fight-or-flight response is enabled in a stressful situation, glycogen (stored sugar) is released from the liver into the bloodstream, which reduces hunger. Also, the stomach tightens, creating a feeling that there is no room for food. The physical result of this is that a person's appetite is reduced. That's why stress causes your friend to turn away from food. So why do you want to stuff yourself in the same situation?

It goes back to those behaviors that you, and so many others, learned in childhood. When you fell down and skinned your knee, your mom may have given you a piece of candy to make you feel better. The mes-sage was that food is comforting, that food can fix you when you're anxious or agitated. Some parents do this a lot; some occasionally. Like-wise, some people grow up to use food as a constant comfort, and some do not. The kind of food you turn to also seems to hark back to your early days. A lot of people reach for sweets because that's what they were offered as kids. Others think of foods like mashed potatoes, meat loaf, or macaroni and cheese as comfort food—homemade foods that suggest the comfort and safety of Mom and home.

People who struggle to control eating, who diet on and off, or who get caught up in diet-binge-diet cycles are susceptible to stress-induced overeating. They are not sensitive to those hunger-reducing cues the body sends out during stress episodes. Stress seems to sap the energy and resolve needed to eat less or control overeating. Bottom line: If you are a dieter, stress probably makes you eat.

Like other eating issues, stress eating is a combination of learned behaviors and the effects of conditions and patterns in daily life. Learning to manage stress in ways other than eating can afford you a multiple payoff. Not only can it help you resolve food and weight struggles, but it can help you feel more balanced within your work, family, and emotional life and generally improve your physical health.

Dieting and Stress

In Chapter Four you read that severe dieting may be a catalyst for low self-esteem, which may, in turn, lead to overeating. In much the same way, dieting may be a stressor that promotes anxiety and leads to overeating. It's not hard to see that a prolonged period of undereating, counting calories, and feeling deprived can make you feel anxious and stressed out. When you add other stress on top of that, your dieting resolve can abruptly break down. At this point the urge to soothe yourself with food cannot be denied. The emotional drain the diet may cause, the resulting feelings of food deprivation, and the added stress combine to trigger a binge. No wonder some studies report that 20 to 40 percent of all women in this country are compulsive eaters at a time when dieting has escalated to new heights.

If you're used to dieting, you're just not going to respond to the natural stress cues that shut down hunger. As a person who's in the habit of controlling food intake, you probably don't respond to internal hunger cues. On a diet you often have to ignore hunger, which means you have to ignore all internal signals, including satiety. So when your body says it's not hungry as a result of stress, you won't hear it.

That's why experts advise against stringent dieting and recommend sensitizing yourself to feelings of hunger and satiety while eating moderately in response to those cues. When you retrain your eating behaviors as you learn to manage emotional triggers—including stress—overeating will become something you used to do.

Tip Sheet

A Fresh Start for Taming Tension

From the beginning of civilization, stress has been a fact of life. Today its sources are as varied as the facets of this technological world. Stress can make you feel bad; it can also make you feel good. But when it becomes overwhelming or when resulting anxiety becomes a constant in your life, stress may cause you to turn to food for relief.

Many people who don't otherwise have serious issues with food report that stress triggers overeating and weight gain for them. For those who have an ongoing battle with compulsive eating, periods of great stress may be their hardest times.

You may not always know what is stressing you out, but you probably do know when you feel stressed. If the cause of your stress is clear, sometimes its solution may also be clear. For instance, a deadline for a tough project at work is looming. Though the pressure is on, you know the end is in sight. You know that you have to work very hard for the next two days and then it will be over. Your emergency-response energy will be expended by the extra-hard effort you put in.

With ongoing or nonspecific stress, you need to take a different approach. You can better prepare your body to cope with stress by getting enough sleep, exercising, eating nutritious low-fat foods, not smoking, and limiting alcohol intake. You can mentally ward off the effects of stress by practicing positive thinking, finding the humor in your life, and having hope and faith in yourself and others. And when the emotions that result from stress hit, use these coping tactics:

❶ Don't Wait to Exhale (or Inhale)

One of the simplest and most effective ways to relax yourself when you are anxious is to spend a few minutes breathing deeply. People who are agitated tend to either hold their breath, take shallow breaths, or overbreathe (hyperventilate), all of which can disrupt the carbon dioxide and oxygen balance in the body and cause further anxiety. Slow, deep breathing can remedy this. It can also help relax your mind with its meditativelike repetition, and your body with the steady expansion and contraction of your stomach and diaphragm.

Instead of reaching for food when anxiety hits, stop and breathe:

1. Inhale slowly and deeply through your nose, feeling your stomach protrude slightly, keeping your chest level.

2. Exhale slowly through your mouth, focusing on the release of breath until your lungs are nearly empty, feeling your stomach slowly contract.

3. Try to sustain a constant in-out rhythm as you gently repeat the process a few times.

❷ Diversionary Tactics

If you've ever been worried about something and then suddenly something diverted your attention, causing you to forget what you were worrying about for a while, you'll understand why many therapists use distraction as a technique to counter anxious eating. By being ready to shift your attention from thoughts of food to something else that's relaxing or pleasurable, you can fend off the compulsion to eat.

Keep a small puzzle, something like a Rubik's Cube, in your purse to turn to when the urge to eat strikes. Carry a riveting novel with you that you can jump right into. Anything that requires you to concentrate and/or use your hands or body can be effective. If your computer is capable, go for a browse on the Web or play a CD-ROM game. Some former overeaters combat night eating by practicing an absorbing hobby in the evenings, such as ceramics or stamp collecting. Get in the habit of distraction and watch your munching habit dissipate.

❸ Communicate Assertively

Stress and anxiety are often the by-products of feeling a lack of control. One way to gain control, to claim the freedom and personal power that are threatened by stressors, is to assert yourself. Being assertive does not mean being aggressive. It means being honest with yourself about your needs and feelings and being able to express them to others in a nonthreatening way.

Interestingly, many who struggle with food and weight issues are not assertive. They are not direct in communicating their needs, acting instead in passive or aggressive ways. They eat to cope with anxiety.

You need to believe, appropriately, that you are entitled to take care of yourself by responding assertively to situations. You need to recognize and share both negative and positive feelings. And you need to accept others' thoughts and feelings about themselves. To communicate assertively:

▶ Be specific and focus on "I" and not "you." Instead of saying, "You always make me feel bad," say, "I feel bad because you said you don't care what I think."

▶ Be active in expressing your needs. Instead of saying, "I was hoping you might help with the kids tonight if you're not too busy," say, "I would like you to watch the kids tonight. I need to take time to finish this report."

▶ Be positively assertive. Express feelings such as "I like it when you cuddle with me" or "I thought you did that very well."

Chapter 7

Are You Hungry or Angry?

"*When I think about how I was when my eating was out of control, I realize that I was mad most of the time," says Jean H., a 46-year-old mother of two, who currently works part time as an image consultant in Los Angeles. "It was like, I walked around in a constant state of being pissed off. But hardly anyone around me knew it. Oh, I guess my husband did, although I didn't really scream and yell at him much. But he knew I was irritated a lot. We didn't talk about it. I usually just got mad inside and then ate. I didn't know what else to do. I couldn't stand feeling that way, and the food always calmed me down—at least for the moment. But afterward I'd just get mad at myself for eating too much, for being overweight, for having no control over myself, you name it. Like I said, I was mad most of the time.*

"Driving in traffic in the city—which I have to do all the time in L.A.—would drive me nuts. My kids got to me a lot, but I knew I couldn't get mad at them. And there'd be times when everything my husband did annoyed me. It's funny, though, because I realize now that I was the angriest at everything around me when I was the angriest at myself. Those were the times I just had no tolerance for anything."

Anger. It seems like a pretty cut-and-dried emotion. Someone or something provokes you, and you're aware of an unpleasant sense of arousal welling up inside you. When the feeling hits, you may cover up the anger in some way; you may vent it toward another person; you may discuss it with someone; or you may try to release it through some action like exercise, screaming, or meditation. You feel anger, and you react. Pretty simple, yes? Not always.

Did you know, for instance, that some people get angry and don't even know it? Along these same lines, did you know that, according to some experts, a depressed person may be an angry person in disguise? In addition, those who experience ongoing underlying anxiety (the kind caused by stress, for example) may unconsciously stifle it by turning it into chronic anger. These examples suggest that as basic an emotion as anger seems to be, its causes, manifestations, and effects are varied and complex.

When it comes to overeating, anger is a powerful contributor and deserving of careful attention. Although you may insist that you don't feel or act angry, the emotion may be bubbling deep down inside. Many clinical psychotherapists who treat compulsive eaters and those with eating disorders attest that anger, even rage, is present in many of their patients.

Of all the emotions you can think of, the one that may have the most intense immediate effect on you, the one that may carry the most negative connotations, and the one that may have the most elusive coping solutions is anger. You may be in the habit of suppressing it so that you don't have to feel its effects or address it causes; or you may be motivated to express it openly, which can be painful and make you feel out of control. In either case, eating can be a convenient fix for these troubling feelings, and even a way to express your anger—more on this later.

As with eating to manage other feelings, habitual eating to stuff anger has its price: weight gain and further anger—at the world in general and at yourself. In the next several pages, you'll learn about the different ways your anger is provoked and revealed. Then you'll be able to use the strategies offered here to weed out unnecessary anger and manage justified anger without food. Once you allow yourself to face these intense feelings, you're on your way to a life free of emotional overeating. It's more than worth the initial distress.

If you don't think you get angry, but you experience unexplained periods of sadness, depression, or irritation, pay careful attention to this chapter. You'll see how anger can be suppressed into other kinds of feelings and why it's possible that you, too, may be using food to hide anger.

Anger Defined

Philosophers and researchers have offered definitions of this complicated emotion for thousands of years. Today anger is generally thought of as a feeling of distress or displeasure, usually accompanied by physiological arousal, that results from some kind of provocation, such as a threat or an injustice. The physical arousal is due to the fight-or-flight response (as explained in Chapter Six) that results from the stress of being provoked. That's

Profile

Name: Becky K.

Location: Idaho

Age: 28

Career: Convenience store manager

Lost: 105 pounds

Not only did exercise help Becky make big strides in her weight loss; it made her a whole new set of friends who share her passion for rock climbing and other activities.

The week before my period, I don't know why, I just feel like eating all the time. Premenstrually, I crave carbohydrates, especially bread. I used to eat *lots* of bread. I know I tend to be emotional at that time, and I find that triggers me to eat more. I'd never paid attention to what and when I was eating until I started tracking my food intake on Weight Watchers. It helped me realize that I was hungrier and eating more during that week. I now know it's not actual hunger but it's *wanting* to eat.

We just never ate healthy when I was growing up. My mother has been overweight as long as I can remember. Usually I wouldn't eat breakfast. I'd go to school and have lunch, then come home starving and pig out, and then have dinner. I've had a weight problem since junior high. I was on the drill team, and our supervisor told me I needed to lose weight, so I was working on it even back then.

I'm what you'd call a "stress eater." Both of my kids were born premature.

One was in the hospital for four months, which caused a lot of stress in my life. At that point I didn't even care about myself—I just ate. I was also in an unhappy marriage. The problems I faced sent my emotions on a roller coaster. At that time I was just trying to get through life day to day. I really couldn't focus on weight loss.

My marriage was based on food and eating. My husband ate a lot, and I had to eat what he ate and make what he liked. We both ate a big dinner and then snacked in front of the TV. He never cared that I was overweight—or at least he didn't complain about it. When I tried to change what we ate, he didn't like it, and I got tired of making different meals for both of us.

I was really bored at home. Just raising the kids and being at home wasn't enough mental stimulation for me, so I ate and I didn't get much exercise.

It was about six or seven months after my divorce that I decided it was my turn to take care of myself. I started worrying about my weight; I knew I was unhealthy. My kids were doing so many things, and at 276 pounds I couldn't keep up with them. I knew they'd only become more active as they got older,

so to keep up with them I decided to lose some weight. That's when I joined Weight Watchers.

At times I've found being lonely still makes me want to eat, and sometimes I still overeat. But I joined a gym, so I

> *"I was really bored at home. Just raising the kids and being at home wasn't enough mental stimulation for me, so I ate and I didn't get much exercise."*

know that I'm exercising and I'm not gaining those 100 pounds back. My best weight-loss advice is to exercise. Now, instead of eating, I'll go and work out. It's hard but you shouldn't give up.

People don't necessarily say mean things to fat people, but they do treat you differently. I feel that I can continue to be successful at losing weight because of the way people react to me now—it keeps me going. I just feel much better about myself.

why you may feel pumped up—breathing may become more rapid and muscles may tighten—when you're in an angry state.

As a result of concentrated studies led by psychologist Charles Spielberger in the late 1970s and early 1980s, it is now widely held that anger should be considered both as a variable emotional state that comes and goes and as a personality trait, one's propensity toward being provoked into angry feelings. This trait anger, which dictates how often you are likely to respond with anger to various situations, has its roots in a number of sources. Studies of twins suggest it may be a genetic propensity, while other research indicates the strong influence that family environment—including levels of support, conflict, and emotional expressiveness you experience throughout your childhood—has on your propensity to get angry.

Jean clearly relates to the concept involving anger and the family. "When I was a kid, it seemed like my father never got angry but my mother did a lot," she remembers. "It was almost as if he frustrated her because he never would fight with her, so she was angry for both of them. On the other hand, my father was an eater, you know? He was heavy, and he ate a lot, and he seemed calm. But I guess he really wasn't so calm. He died of a heart attack when he was 60. It seems like I got some of my 'stuff' from both of them. I'd get mad a lot, like my mom, and I'd eat to calm down, like my dad. Recognizing this was a real breakthrough for me. It played a part in helping me get past my own overeating thing."

It's important to point out that anger is not all bad. True, it can and does lead to unhappy consequences, such as distorted thinking, negative coping habits (such as excessive drinking or eating), and physical and psychological health problems (examples are high blood pressure and chronic hostility). But there are, in fact, situations that provoke justifiable anger, and the appropriate expression of this kind of anger can have positive results:

- ▶ It can be liberating and esteem-boosting.

- ▶ It can result in greater physical energy.

- ▶ It can send a message to the person who incited the anger that changes need to be made.

- ▶ It can relieve inner tension and even promote better health.

The key words here are *appropriate expression* of your anger. Overreacting to minor annoyances, ranting and railing, eating to quash the feelings—these results are not generally appropriate. Later in the chapter you'll find ways to modulate, respond to, and release your anger.

Is Your Anger Overt or Suppressed?

When a situation provokes your anger, your course of action will generally go in one of two directions: you will express it overtly, or you will suppress it. Both of these expressions of anger have their own variations.

Although it might seem that overt, or outward, expression of anger is always a healthy option, this is not always the case. Overt expression in the form of verbal attacks on others is hardly ever positive. The angry person may feel a sort of relief from this, but the relief will probably be temporary. Experts say that those who vent anger in this way ultimately get angrier, not less angry. Recent studies indicate that venting anger by screaming or yelling at another serves to elevate, not lower, heart rate and blood pressure. In addition, recipients of this kind of wrath are generally affected adversely, making them much less likely to cooperate in resolving the cause of the anger.

Overt anger can have positive results, however, when the angry person reacts by discussing her feelings with either the person who is the source of the anger or another person. People who use this method of anger expression tend to have lower blood pressure than those who vent with hostility or suppress their anger. Also, *controlled* discussion with the person who is the anger catalyst is more likely to lead to a resolution to the anger than is a hostile interchange.

Suppressed anger is generally anger that is held inside. This may mean that you keep the feelings to yourself, or it may mean that you repress the feelings to the point that you are not even conscious of them. Suppression of anger seems to be more of an issue for women than for men, probably because society has long discouraged the outward expression of anger by females (more on this in the next section). Like overt anger, suppression of anger is not all negative or positive. When a person is prone to reacting with angry feelings toward every frustration, it may be in her interest to assume more responsibility for her feelings by "controlling" or suppressing certain anger episodes. On the other hand, keeping all angry feelings down by stifling the feelings in some way is not in a person's best interests. Chronically repressed anger may show up as other, more "acceptable" conditions, such as excessive worry or depression.

Interestingly, research indicates that both overt and suppressed anger can lead to health issues such as headaches, tension, high blood pressure, and substance abuse—including overeating.

Depression—The Flip Side of Anger?

Depression—a mood disorder characterized by sadness and lethargy—is certainly not the same thing as anger, but some psychoanalysts and researchers believe that depression is anger turned inward. Some believe that depression can be a consequence of repressed anger (or anger that is not expressed overtly). They have found that depressed people exhibit inward hostility and resentment. Conversely, some studies reveal that depressed women do, indeed, vent anger. One such study shows that depressed women who vented anger were more depressed than those who did not.

Although the tide of thought about the relationship between anger and depression is turning, it remains clear that the two emotional states are linked. Research has consistently shown that trait anger—one's propensity toward being provoked into angry feelings—is at a high level in depressed individuals. A major study on women and anger from the University of Tennessee at Knoxville supports these findings and also shows that the more women discuss their anger in a reasonable way, the less likely they are to experience depression.

The Way Women Get Angry

Expression of anger and ways of coping with it have been dictated by society for hundreds of years. Perhaps this is because anger has consistently been viewed as a strong negative emotion that needs to be controlled. From the 18th century through the mid-19th century, men, women, and children were taught to suppress angry feelings to promote family harmony. It wasn't until this century that analysts and researchers espoused the view that anger should be expressed openly for positive therapeutic results.

Still, there seems to be a marked difference between the way men and women handle anger. While it's inaccurate to say that all men express anger overtly and all women suppress anger, many believe that the societal cues are clear. Little girls are taught that expressing anger is not appropriate while little boys are encouraged to do so. Anger clearly is an unfeminine trait. It seems that men are supposed to get mad, and women are supposed to get sad. It's not surprising that many women report crying as an effect of anger (far fewer men report that they cry when angry).

Research also suggests variations in the issues that motivate men and women to anger. One study suggests that interpersonal experiences are the prime force behind anger reactions for females, while performance evaluation causes males to anger most. The University of Tennessee Women's Anger Study supports this finding, adding that the interpersonal relationships within a woman's family are her key anger triggers, followed by interpersonal encounters in the workplace. The study also shows that the next most common trigger for a woman's anger after the interpersonal realm is the intrapersonal realm, or herself.

It appears that a woman's unmet expectations about those close to her, herself, and society in general are the primary catalysts for her anger. Part of the anger that her own self provokes has to do with her self-esteem. Personal failures, being treated disrespectfully, and stigmatization by society are self-esteem issues that provoke anger. (Recall how esteem issues such as these affect eating behavior, as discussed in Chapter Four.)

A woman's anger, then, is tied into the very crux of her being. By the same token, ineffective expression of her anger can affect her in powerful ways.

Why Anger Leads to Eating

Everyone gets angry, and some studies suggest that many people experience anger often and intensely. If you think you don't have a problem with anger, that may indeed be true. But realize that the expression of anger is not always overt and obvious. Anger may quickly turn into sadness and tears; anger may be transformed into a low-level depression; anger may be suppressed and not felt at all because of the societal dictate that it is an inappropriate emotion.

If you've been taught that anger is an unacceptable emotional response, you might turn to food to soothe the rage. For instance, if something makes you angry and rage slowly but surely wells up and grows within you, you may use food to stuff the feelings down. Likewise, if you feel that you're losing control when you get angry, you may eat to stabilize yourself. In this way you stifle angry feelings, stop them from being vented outwardly, and thus believe that you are maintaining control. Conversely, when your anger is already suppressed into sadness, depression, or the incapacity to feel it at all, eating may serve as a way to express the anger: "I'll show you! I'll eat and get fat!"

Overall, a person who is prone to eat for comfort will likely eat to manage anger. Remember, too, that anger may induce a physical stress response, another catalyst for the emotional eater to turn to food.

The Eat-Anger-Eat Cycle

As is the case with eating to deal with other feelings, anger eating often backfires. Whether a person chronically eats to stuff overt feelings or to vent suppressed feelings, the result eventually is more anger. Consider the possibilities:

▶ You become angry at yourself for being weak and unable to control your eating.

▶ You become angry at the world for telling you that being overweight means you're an inferior person.

▶ You become angry at those close to you because your ongoing anger magnifies your reaction to petty annoyances, especially the actions of the people you live with.

Anger is a complicated emotion. Sometimes its causes are difficult to pinpoint and address head on. For the emotional eater it is easier to temporarily cope with the anger of overeating by eating more. Ironically, many women in the throes of overeating do not think anger is a part of why they stuff themselves. When asked if anger is an issue for them, they report that they do not get angry much, if at all. Perhaps the social pattern of anger suppression in women, combined with the numbing effect of too much food, serves to erase those angry feelings from a woman's consciousness. On the other hand, therapists report that overeaters who are in the midst of counseling are more able to see the link between anger and eating in their behavior—and the painful consequences of this behavior.

As with the issues of low self-esteem and stress, anger can provoke people to eat, which can lead to more anger and more eating. If you take away the food, you might be left with some pretty powerful feelings. But these feelings need to be and can be managed in healthy ways.

The Lessons of Anger

Allowing yourself to experience anger, to go through the initial distress and the aftermath of feelings such as guilt, misery, and depletion, seems like a pretty agonizing prospect. Eating to quell anger is a habitual reaction that minimizes the immediate pain. Yet anger eating, as already discussed, has its own set of agonizing consequences. If this, combined with the other health ramifications of anger, is not enough to entice you to develop alternative anger-management techniques, consider this thought: when you stop to listen to your anger and examine its provocations, you will hear messages that can help you find a new way of looking at and dealing with your whole life.

▶ Your anger can tell you that your level of stress is exceeding your physical and mental capacity to cope effectively. It can show you where you need to simplify and improve your life.

▶ Your anger can tell you that there is something problematic in a relationship, which needs to be corrected.

▶ Your anger can teach you what you value most in life and what your priorities are.

▶ Your anger can show you when your rights are being threatened and that you are justified in taking action to correct this.

For Jean the best thing about dealing with anger without food was the boost to her self-esteem. "When I forced myself to tough out those feelings, I realized that some of what I was mad about was trivial, and some of it was important stuff that I had to look at. Eventually, and it took some time, I realized that I didn't have to get so angry about the little stuff because it just sort of came and went. But I found out it was okay to get angry about the big stuff. All in all, I feel so much more in control because I'm dealing with anger in a good way and I'm not eating to make it go away."

Tip Sheet

Your Anger Manager

Like stress, anger results from your perception that something is threatening or unjust. These perceptions can be colored by an array of factors, including your family history, cultural mores, the media, your life experiences, your habits—and certainly your moods. For instance, ever notice how a bad driver can make you furious on one day, while on another day the same situation won't much bother you?

If little things often set you off, it's worth stopping for a moment to examine the cause of the anger. Is it really a threat or an injustice that affects your life in a big way? Or has your anger been too easily aroused? By simply noticing when you are provoked by a serious issue as opposed to a trivial one, you can begin to abort unnecessary anger episodes. Remember that overt venting isn't always good for you.

Initial feelings of anger are a knee-jerk reaction to a thought or event, but reacting in an angry way is voluntary, a conscious choice you make based on the way you evaluate a situation. Ask yourself if an irritating condition is worthy of real anger. The realization that you may be overreacting can help you choose to let the anger go. Two tools can help you make choices when you're at the crossroads of anger: perspective and humor.

If, on the other hand, challenges to your value system and sense of justice seem to get no rise out of you, there's a good chance you are in the habit of stuffing or denying anger. For example, if you are underpaid for your work compared to others at your experience and productivity level, if you work outside the home and then get no help from your spouse with household chores and child care, if your children continually push your authority to the limit, you probably should be angry. Allowing yourself to feel anger in instances such as these is appropriate because these feelings indicate the need to take action. Taking this anger to the next step, such as rationally discussing it with another person—even the person causing the anger—is an appropriate expression of the anger and can lead you to solutions. (See tip 3, "Communicate Assertively," in Chapter Six for an effective discussion technique.)

Along with the strategies explained above, here are three more great ways to help you cope with anger: one to use when anger hits, one to strengthen your overall defenses, and one to quell the anger juices in the first place. All can help you stop using food to cope with anger.

❶ Find Some Alone Time

When anger hits with full force, take some time to isolate yourself and cool off. Lying on your bed, walking outside, or doing yoga stretches for a few minutes will do the trick. Avoid intense exercise. Though some people work out to dissipate anger, new research out of Case Western Reserve University in Cleveland shows that this may exacerbate the feelings by stimulating you even more.

Once you've calmed down, you can determine the cause of your anger and decide if it's worth working out in discussion.

❷ Tap into Your Spirituality

When a woman's sense of personal power, values, or ideals is threatened in some way, she may be provoked to anger. As suggested, the anger wells up from the very core of her being, the place where her sense of self is challenged.

Strengthening yourself at this core is an important way to steel yourself against anger provocation. And a powerful way to do this is to focus on and nurture your spirituality, whatever that may be to you. A strong connection with your source of spirituality can promote inner peace, a greater sense of yourself and your place in the world, and your uniqueness. It can bolster your value system so that you are less susceptible to feeling disappointed or threatened.

Spend some time each week in church or temple or just meditating or reading by yourself to promote your spiritual connection. You'll get the added bonus of some extra moments of calm.

③ Slow Down

It's called hurry sickness: a condition caused when you become caught up in the traps of too little time and too much technology. The result is that you do too much too fast, leading to impatience and resulting anger with the world and yourself. In a way, it's a kind of perfectionist attitude; if things don't go quickly and smoothly, you get ticked off.

The cure for hurry sickness is to take life at a slower pace. You need to organize your priorities so that you can accomplish the most important things in your life and let go of the rest if they don't get done "yesterday." You need to stop and realize what means the most to you, perhaps your family, your friends, and your health. Then consciously decide to downshift your everyday pace so that you can enjoy your life more and so that you won't be in such a hurry—or in such a snit when things don't go your way. Less hurry = less anger.

Chapter 8

Boredom and Loneliness: Filling Up the Empty Holes

"*I'm pretty much of a loner,*" *says Bill S., who is 49, single, and lives in Astoria, New York. "I actually like being alone. I like being around people too, but I revel in the fact that I'm responsible only to myself. Sure, I get lonely and bored. In terms of eating, I think I was especially affected by boredom. I ate because I was alone and I had nothing else to do. And when I ate, I ate a lot. Food has always been an indulgence for me, instant gratification. It was my way of doing what I wanted when I wanted, without anyone else to tell me what I could or couldn't do. I was sated by that feeling of comfort, of eating however much I wanted when I wanted it.*

"When I'm at home alone, I turn on the TV. TV is my company. Before I started changing the way I eat, the TV was on a lot, and I ate a lot. And, of course, there were all of those commercials telling you to eat this and drink that. It was like, if somebody poured a cup of coffee on TV, I had to have a cup of coffee. I was very susceptible to those triggers. I was alone, sometimes I was bored, I watched TV, and I ate. I didn't feel good when I was eating too much."

Boredom and loneliness often go hand in hand. They are not the same thing, but they are linked by several common factors, especially when over-eating enters the equation. In both there is a feeling that something is missing. With boredom it is a lack of stimulating activity; with loneliness it is a lack of meaningful interpersonal relationships. The two states are often, but not necessarily, experienced in tandem. Research indicates that they trigger more people (women and men, overweight or not) to eat than do other nonhunger issues. They are distinct from other emotional states in that they produce, in their purest forms, minimal physical arousal. (Loneliness may, however, trigger other emotions and the intense feelings that accompany them.) This means that the feelings can be vague—less about emotional angst, more about a dull sense of emptiness. This also suggests that relief for boredom and loneliness is not so much about calming down but rather about filling up.

What these two conditions have in common with other eating triggers is the way they are shaped by your perceptions. Like esteem issues, stress, and anger, boredom and loneliness are colored by how you perceive and react to various situations. For example, you might be totally absorbed as you work on a complex jigsaw puzzle, while another person might be totally bored by it. In a situation such as this, there's a good chance your thoughts will not turn to food. Another example: a co-worker may revel in the social stimulation of your workplace; you may feel isolated and lonely in the same environment. Feeling this way may lead you to habitual snacking at work.

Loneliness seems, perhaps, the more troublesome of these two states and the more difficult to remedy. But if you eat out of boredom, you know that it, too, is a compelling catalyst. Both loneliness and boredom result when basic human needs are not met, and it is all too easy to turn to food to manage these needs. But, and it can't be said too often, the food fix is a temporary coping measure that is fraught with its own problems. Food does not make you less bored or lonely for very long. It can, however, lead you away from real solutions for these conditions and toward further isolation, boredom, and loneliness. This chapter will help you understand the nature of these states so that you can address them head-on with the right courses of action.

Caught Up in the Doldrums

Everyone experiences boredom. It's that feeling of discontent that sweeps over you because nothing around you seems interesting or worthwhile. Maybe there's nothing to do—or maybe everything there is to do is tedious. You may regularly feel bored during a specific time period, such as after dinner at home. Or you may feel bored most of the time because there isn't enough activity in your life.

Why do people become bored? Human beings need variety and stimulation in their lives. When these needs are not sufficiently met, boredom can result. Humans also have a natural curiosity that needs to be sparked and satisfied. Boredom may occur when this drive is not faced with engaging challenges. Remember that individual perceptions come into play here. A certain activity may seem interesting, different, or challenging to one person but dull to the next.

When boredom is chronic, when it regularly pervades your life, it may be difficult to recognize. You don't have the distinct physiological arousal that accompanies other emotional states to tip you off to its presence. It may be masked by an ongoing sense of flatness in your life. It may, however, reveal itself in symptomatic behavior, such as when you feel:

▶ Tired or drowsy

▶ Depressed

▶ Noncommittal about making plans or setting goals

▶ Restless

▶ Compelled to eat when you're not hungry

Eating to alleviate boredom shows, perhaps more clearly than with any other feelings state, how much of a habit eating when you're not hungry can become. Boredom does not bring on a state of high arousal, as do most emotions. The seemingly uncontrollable urge to stuff down the feelings, then, is not present. Yet boredom eating is a common phenomenon. Many people turn to food whenever they are bored, with no thought of alternative behaviors. Why?

Again, as is the case with other overeating issues, society plays a role in the reason. Eating is a highly acceptable, even encouraged, remedy for boredom. For instance, in workplaces where jobs are tedious, such as factories, regulated coffee breaks are promoted. If you work at an office, your boss would probably frown on your reading the newspaper or working a puzzle at your desk but not mind you snacking there during the day. Watching TV, the American boredom-fighting pastime, just doesn't seem complete to most people without a snack to go along with it.

There is an upside to the boredom scenario. If you recognize when you feel bored and can pinpoint the times and situations when boredom is likely to occur, you should have a relatively easy time alleviating boredom and bored eating. If you suspect that boredom is more a chronic condition in your life (the symptoms listed on the preceding page may help you to recognize it), you may have to put in a bit more effort to shake yourself out of it. In either case, the strategies offered at the end of this chapter can help you combat boredom without food.

A Craving for Companionship

Just as boredom indicates a need for worthwhile activity in your life, loneliness results from a need for significant human contact. Pioneering researcher Frieda Fromm-Reichman described loneliness as "the longing for interpersonal intimacy." This five-word definition speaks volumes, especially for women, who generally place far more importance on relationships than do men. (Men, as a rule, prioritize independence and achievement ahead of interpersonal connection.) This is not to say that men do not get lonely. But far more women report grappling with loneliness—and eating to soothe its ache.

The roots of loneliness are in the lack of sufficient interpersonal experience. The pure feeling is one of emptiness, a dull inner craving or ache. But the state of loneliness creates a sort of vacuum, which other feelings may rush in to fill. For example, your loneliness may cause you to feel unhappy because you are alone and without a sense of connection to others. Your unhappiness may be furthered by a realization that you are not taking responsibility for your current state. Other feelings, such as the pain of low self-worth, fear of continued aloneness, or the anxiety of feeling trapped, can come raging to the surface when you are

Diary of a Bored Housewife

It's entirely possible to be very busy and very bored at the same time. Consider, for instance, the case of one stay-at-home mom with three young children. She married young and worked as a manufacturer's sales representative until she had her first child. She and her husband agreed that she would quit her job and focus on raising their children. Although she enjoyed her work, she really wanted to be at home full-time with her family.

She loves being a mom and being there for her kids. Even so, she feels stuck in a rut. The routine is getting the best of her: taking the kids here and there, running errands, doing housework, cooking, and feeling like every day is exactly the same. Basically, she is bored. She feels tired most of the time. She eats whenever she is alone, just to make herself feel better. In the past few years she has gained about 30 pounds, and that makes her very unhappy. And yet she continues to eat out of boredom.

This story is not unusual. Here is a woman who knows she's doing an important thing by nurturing her children. But the sameness of each day, the limited excitement in her life, and perhaps even a silent wish to be doing something else have created a state of boredom. She has plenty to do. She just doesn't feel mentally challenged. Her life lacks that crucial element of variety that is a human imperative.

Moms who juggle the responsibilities of outside work plus home and child care may have more than their fair share of resulting stress. Stay-at-home moms must grapple with a different and perhaps more insidious adversary, boredom. As with stress, eating becomes an easy, albeit temporary coping method.

Women who do not work outside the home need to find ways to shake up their routine as well as add intellectual challenges to their life. If this is your story:

▶ For mental stimulation, take a night class in an area of interest or do volunteer work that taps skills you do not use at home (artistic talent, salesmanship, or writing ability, to name a few).

▶ To change your routine, carve out some time each week to have an adult "play date" with friends. Together, go to a museum one week, a foreign film the next, have a massage the next.

▶ To plan truly free time, suggest swapping baby-sitting time with another stay-at-home mom. Then sit in the park and people-watch, wander in your favorite department store, or simply sit and sip a cappuccino for a good hour.

When you change your environment and activities in small ways such as these, you'll make a big dent in your level of boredom and the resulting need to nurture yourself with extra food.

alone and lonely. Lengthy periods of isolation can also contribute to chronic stress.

Feeling connected—to others, to oneself, to a sense of purpose—is a human necessity. Numerous studies suggest that without it, physical health deteriorates, longevity is affected adversely, and destructive habits, including overeating, can set in. Many people feel lonely at times, and that's okay. It's when loneliness takes a lead role in your life that something has to give.

In Bill's case he often chose to be alone. He enjoyed his solitude and independence. But when he was overeating, he had less respect for himself and was more prone to eating out of boredom and loneliness. "My weight was definitely holding me back from making intimate connections with people. As I get older and mellower, I sometimes wish I had someone to share my life with. Now that I've changed my attitude about food and eating with the help of Weight Watchers, I'm starting to feel better about myself. I suspect I'll be more inclined to seek out a relationship with someone."

Certainly there are times when social isolation is imposed upon you, such as when you move to a new town, experience the death of a spouse or breakup of a relationship. The loneliness you experience from conditions such as these is natural. Eventually these situations will evolve, and with some effort on your part, you will walk through the lonely times and emerge with renewed connection to others and yourself. But if you stay stuck in a pattern of isolation, if loneliness becomes chronic, if you habitually use food to fill up the social void, you need to make some changes in your lifestyle.

Before you do, however, it's important to understand that being lonely is not the same thing as being alone. Loneliness does not need to happen whenever you are by yourself. Yes, you need nurturing relationships with others, both in your personal life and in the workplace, where you may spend a good chunk of your time. But solitude need not be a negative experience. In fact, it can be highly rewarding, in that it allows you to nurture that very important relationship with the person you're closest to—yourself.

Just as you can be alone without being lonely, you can feel lonely among friends, lonely at work, and lonely in a marriage. You may have many people in your life, but these relationships may not always provide the significant and satisfying interpersonal connection that is your human need. Says Stanford University School of Medicine mind-body researcher Kenneth R. Pelletier, M.D., "A lack of connection to others in a social support system may be symptomatic of a lack of connection within oneself." If you don't nurture a healthy relationship with yourself, based on a positive view of yourself and your actions, intimacy with others may be difficult to achieve.

Why Are You Lonely?

Most people feel lonely either because they do not have enough significant relationships or because they do not get enough satisfaction from the relationships they have. In both cases there is a lack of feeling connected to others. You don't have to have food issues to have loneliness issues. But overeaters are often plagued by loneliness. Here are some reasons why.

> ▶ "I'm unlovable." If you think you're weak or bad because you cannot control your food and/or weight, it may follow that you feel unworthy of being loved. The result is that you may not seek out relationships for fear that people will not like you

Profile

Name: Beverly K.

Location: California

Age: 46

Career: Client service representative

Lost: 37 pounds

Making nights when she has a Weight Watchers meeting a girls' night out makes meetings something to look forward to for Beverly.

I was the middle child of five children, and at a young age I learned to keep things bottled up inside and turned to food for comfort. I guess my issues with food and weight started when I was a teenager. When I was about 13, I started putting on weight. It was only a few pounds in the beginning, but it escalated over time. It seems I was always struggling to lose 10 pounds on some diet or other. Usually I'd gain it back, plus more.

My mother was heavy; four of the five kids in our family had weight problems; and my grandmother was almost 300 pounds before she died. There is a pattern of overeating and weight problems in our family. We always had lots of sweets in our house.

I was withdrawn—it was partly my personal makeup and partly because of the way my mother treated me. I withdrew even more because I didn't like the way I looked. My mother never thought I could do anything right. My weight was just another failed area of my life. So I thought that if I didn't make waves I wouldn't get into trouble with her or anyone. I could just fade into the background, into my own little world. Food was my comfort. As an adult, I turned to food whenever I was dealing with fears, stress, or people being upset with me. I couldn't confront others, so I turned away from them and toward food. I ate to bury emotions I couldn't deal with. I was basically a closet eater, doing it when no one else was around. I hid candy in my drawers at home; even my husband didn't know.

One thing I did find security in was my work. I excelled there, so I felt accepted and successful in at least one area of my life. But my overeating had become a bad habit, like an addiction. So even when I felt better about myself, I was still eating a lot of sweets.

As my weight increased over the years, it was another area of my life that I couldn't control—another failure. Many times I'd get angry and not know how to deal with it. My mother got angry and took it out on us kids. I didn't want to act like that, so I basically didn't deal with my anger. I just stuffed it down with food.

In 1992 I decided to go to Weight Watchers. I was 30 pounds overweight and very unhappy. At first I used the program only as a diet. I persevered and did well, but in reality I was just dieting again and wasn't in the mindset of really changing my habits or myself. When the holidays came around, I just started overeating again, and I gained all the weight back.

I was embarrassed to go back to Weight Watchers. I felt I had failed. It took me awhile to feel ready to try it again. But in August 1996 I started going to meetings with a friend. It was great, and it worked. The leader was wonderful too. It became a girls' night out *and* a good meeting. In April 1997

> **" I was basically a closet eater, doing it when no one else was around. I hid candy in my drawers at home; even my husband didn't know."**

I reached my goal: I lost 37 pounds. My friend and I are still going to meetings together.

I have learned to find different ways to deal with my emotions. Now I write down my feelings to release them instead of trying to eat them away. I didn't communicate before. Now I try to talk things out with my husband when there's a problem. It helps me focus on where I'm at. I wrote a letter to myself about how I felt when I was heavy. Every once in a while, I read it as a reinforcement for why I took the weight off. It helps me stay on track.

I see things clearly now. I know that food isn't going to solve my problems. I might take a nice hot bath or work out when I feel stressed instead of eating. I focus more on the positive aspects of my life. I've also learned to pat myself on the back. I no longer feel that I fail at everything. I can succeed. I do succeed.

◆ ◆ ◆

anyway. You may also, either consciously or subconsciously, hold existing relationships at a superficial level—if they knew you better they would not like you. Whether by keeping people away or keeping those around you from getting too close, you support your loneliness.

▶ "I can't trust anyone." Feeling negative about yourself often leads to negative thinking about others. If you've been "burned" in the past or someone has disappointed you, you may figure it's bound to happen again. So why make new friends?

▶ "I'm afraid to meet new people." When confidence is shaky, taking even small risks, such as starting a conversation can be intimidating. Thus the potential for making new friends is diminished.

▶ "Nobody understands me." How could they possibly know what you're going through? And if they did, they'd probably reject you. So you just don't share that kind of intimacy with people.

▶ "I'd rather be alone." If you're in the throes of overeating, you want to eat in private. So you isolate yourself.

All of these attitudes share a common theme: when you don't feel good about yourself, when your self-esteem is flagging, you may keep others at arm's-length and yourself in a state of loneliness. The cure for loneliness needs to start at your own center. Nurturing a healthy intrapersonal relationship, based on self-respect, will help you to value and encourage deeper connections with other people. At the end of this chapter, you'll find techniques for doing this.

When Food Is Your Best Friend

It's easy to understand why many people find that eating is the answer to boredom, loneliness, or a combination of the two. Eating and food preparation are time-consuming activities that can fill up empty hours. Food is easy to access; it's pretty much there for you whenever you "need" it. It makes no particular demands on you. It can hold your interest for a period of time. It can offer you a sense of comfort and even love. In other words, it may seem like the optimal kind of friend—the friend that asks nothing of you but gives you what you need. But is it?

Most often, no. Eating to fill up times of boredom or the emptiness of loneliness can become a problem habit. Not only does it lead to the discomfort of uncontrolled food consumption, the pain of weight gain, and overall guilt, but it promotes further boredom and loneliness. Bored eating inhibits you from seeking stimulating activity that would prevent boredom. Lonely eating contributes to a sense of isolation that promotes further loneliness. As with so many examples of emotional eating, the fix becomes the cause.

"Having another person in my life is not the driving force of my life," says Bill. "But I do want to feel good about myself. I'm alone, and right now I like that. Now that I've changed my attitude about food and the way I eat, I feel better about myself and I have more energy. I like that too. Instead of watching too much TV and eating too much, I sit down at the piano and play or do other things of interest to me. My whole life is better, whether I'm alone or with people."

If you want to stop overeating, if you are tired of using food as a temporary measure to cope with feelings such as boredom and loneliness, you can change your behavior. However, you have to give yourself permission to change. Why permission? Developing new habits isn't always easy. It takes time, it takes effort, and it takes the ability to fail, forgive yourself, and try again. You have to permit yourself to try something that might at first seem harder than eating. Yes, eating to manage emotions is easy. But the aftereffects, as you already know, can be very, very hard. To get to the other side of overeating means you have to look at your life in a new way, be honest about what motivates you to eat too much, and work on changing yourself. Many people have done it. They know how worthwhile the process is. You will too.

Tip Sheet

A New Inner Life

If you eat when you are bored, lonely, or both, don't be too hard on yourself. Realize that some boredom or loneliness is natural. It's when they escalate and you fall into a rut of emptiness that problems occur. You have more control over these conditions than you may realize. Of all the psychological and emotional triggers for overeating, these two states may be the easiest to change. That's because you already have the very tool that can turn boredom into interest and loneliness into involvement—your thinking.

Boredom often comes when your thought processes—your intelligence, if you will—are not challenged. But if you turn the process around, you can look at boredom as a challenge in itself and use your intelligent thinking to alleviate it. How? By discovering ways to make stimulating changes in your life, by researching mind-flexing activities that offer you a sense of accomplishment, and by learning about new things that will satisfy your natural curiosity and human need for variety.

Your present way of thinking may also be making you lonely. Making snap judgments about people, assuming no one can love you because you are overweight, and expecting problems in relationships because that's what happened in the past—these are all ways of thinking that can keep you from developing satisfying interpersonal connections. In addition, a belief that being alone is the same as being lonely can inhibit your ability to nurture that all-important relationship with yourself. These thoughts promote social isolation. Replacing them with positive thinking about developing friendships and being alone can help you banish loneliness from your life.

Try to be more aware of your "automatic" thinking in social or solitary situations. If you find that a negative thought is leading you away from interpersonal contact, replace it with a more productive one. For example, change "He won't like me anyway" to "Maybe we have something in common to talk about." If you're alone at night and apt to think, "Another boring night by myself," replace the idea with something like "I'm going to sign up for that art class on Tuesday nights."

The way you think and feel about yourself affects your inclination to be bored and lonely. A person who values herself will seek a life filled with stimulation and connection to others. It's about nurturing healthy self-esteem. Reread the tips on social support and volunteering at the end of Chapter Four. They will not only help you bolster your self-worth but also help you walk away from boredom and loneliness and toward a richer life. Both strategies offer behavior that can replace overeating, as do the ideas suggested below.

❶ Take a "Juice" Break

Not everything you do in life can be stimulating. Sometimes you just have to do things that are boring. Daily paperwork at the office and regular household chores can turn into a rut that leads to mindless eating. Instead of pulling that bag of chips out of your desk drawer or working your way through a bowl of candy as you dust and vacuum, inject some stimulation into the chore time.

▶ Get up and move for a few minutes. Try a short walk, ten jumping jacks, or some deep breathing and a stretch out in the fresh air. Physical activity is by its very nature an antidote for boredom.

▶ Seek human contact. Chat with a co-worker for a few minutes. Or call a friend or your mate for a five-minute shmooze. Ask her or him to share a funny or interesting part of the day with you. Enjoy the "company" and refresh your spirit.

▶ Build in a challenge. Set a tight time limit on a report you have to complete; try to get your heart rate up to an aerobic level as you do housework. Be creative and think of other ways to pump up humdrum tasks. In this way you up the ante and turn a boring activity into one with more edge. More edge, less ennui.

One more related tip: Try to do the work in a place where food is not easily accessible, if at all possible. If you're at home, keep easy-to-grab snack foods out of sight and reach.

❷ Cultivate Solitary Pleasures

When you think about it, there are probably many things you like to do by yourself. You don't need another person's company to write in your journal, plant flowers in your garden, or read a good book. Being alone and enjoying solitary activities can be a very happy experience. It can also promote your appreciation of your own company.

Make a list of everything you enjoy doing alone. When you find yourself on your own and bored or lonely, read the list and remind yourself that you have the time and opportunity to do something wonderful for yourself. Then pick one thing and do it. Here's some help getting your list started.

1. Dancing alone in my living room to _____ music.

2. Sitting in the park with the sun on my face.

3. Going in-line skating.

4. Surfing the Web for funky new sites.

5. Playing with clay.

6. _____

7. _____

8. _____

9. _____

10. _____

③ Find Your Passion

Adolph Adler, a founder of early psychiatry, advocated that each person has a creative self, an innate quality that enables her to take responsibility for her own life and become autonomous. A lonely person may unwittingly become overly self-absorbed. The creative self can lead a person away from egocentricity and toward real care and concern for others—and herself. It's about having an internal life and creatively seeking something to feel passionate about. When a person develops a passionate interest, her enthusiasm acts like a magnet that draws others with similar passions toward her. She has something that she can feel excited about, something to fill her soul as well as her time.

It's one thing to do things you like doing (see tip 2 above). It's another thing to find an interest that has real sustaining power. Longtime collectors—of stamps, books, antiques, whatever—are prime examples of people with a passionate interest. You may love to paint landscapes, work in an animal shelter, read short stories, or design stained-glass projects. Open your mind to all kinds of possibilities, find a passionate pursuit, and don't be surprised when boredom and loneliness—and eating to deal with them—become a nonissue for you.

Chapter 9

Changing for Life

Having read through the last eight chapters, you know that this is a book about why people overeat and how to help change the behavior. You also know that this is not a book about dieting; it is not about starving; it is not about trying to "white-knuckle" your way through your urge to eat. It is about understanding the outside and inside forces that compel people to turn to food for comfort. It is about recognizing your particular eating triggers, both circumstantial and emotional, and learning about alternative coping behaviors. It is about breaking old, painful habits and developing new, productive ones.

Each chapter has focused on a specific issue; combined, they offer a package of factors in a person's life that are most germane to struggles with food and weight. They provide you with insights and strategies you can use to help change your problem behaviors. You now have all the pieces of the puzzle. But how do you put them together? What provides the glue that makes the pieces become one cohesive whole with staying power? In other words, how do you achieve lasting change?

It's time for the big picture, the final phase that will help you break your emotional-eating pattern and become the healthy, positive person you want to be. The key words are "lasting change." When it comes to your emotional makeup and ingrained habits, change is not simply about deciding to do something and then doing it. Change is a process. It is first about readiness, then action, then maintenance. It takes some time, some thought, and some motivation—commodities that you already have. Now you need the method. Read on.

The Power of State of Mind

Have you ever noticed the difference that being in a good mood or a bad mood can make when you set out to do something? When you feel positive, content, happy, and upbeat, work is more pleasant, chores are less taxing, time seems to fly by—you may even experience an abundance of energy. If you're in a blue, angry, sour, or hopeless mindset, however, a day at work can seem endless, and you get little accomplished; cleaning the house seems like an impossibility. In fact, everything seems harder to do.

This overall mood that is so changeable is your state of mind. It is the way you are thinking, feeling, and then reacting physically—the way you stand and breathe, for example—at any given time. The things you experience in your daily life plus your thoughts and memories can trigger changes in your state of mind, changes that may be frequent and abrupt. Consider this scenario: You have just awakened from a pleasant dream. You feel happy, relaxed, there's a spring in your step as you enjoy breathing the fresh morning air. You look forward to a light breakfast of fresh fruit and toast. Then you get the morning paper and read a disturbing piece of news, and all at once your mood darkens. You feel tired, less hopeful. You're suddenly craving a rich breakfast pastry.

By simply reading the newspaper, your state of mind changed dramatically. Your first mood was upbeat, elicited from pleasant associations you had from a nice pre-awakening dream. This positive state allowed your inner assets of energy and joy to forge to the surface. You were primed for success. But when your state became negative after experiencing the morning news, your mental attitude and physical strength suffered. At that moment your inner assets, or resources, were no longer working for you. In order for you to feel better and more ready to proceed positively, your state will have to change again.

Prologue: Getting Anchored

You don't have to wait and hope that something you associate with good feelings will miraculously happen. You can create your own effective trigger, or anchor, that will change your state of mind, call up your inner resources, and ready you to face challenges and make positive changes in your life. This process is called *anchoring*. It is a way that you can, whenever you choose, trigger yourself into a state of mind that will help you achieve your goals. The anchors are things in your life that, either through repetition or through a single emotional instance, cause you to make associations that put you in various emotional states.

Anchors can be positive, such as the song you associate with your first love, or negative, such as the sight of a hypodermic needle. They can be thoughts ("I'm a smart person"; "He's a jerk!"), sounds (your mother's voice;

a siren), smells (apple pie; smoke), sights (a red traffic light; a field of flowers), words (grandmother; test; genitals), and physical conditions (a warm, sunny day; being enclosed in a small closet). An anchor is anything that puts a person in a particular state of mind.

Because change can be challenging, sometimes even frightening, being in a resourceful state of mind makes all the difference in achieving it. Whether you want to stop isolating yourself and join a support group or talk out your anger instead of eating over it, using an anchor first to achieve a positive state can make any behavior change easier to accomplish. Here's an example of how to do it.

1. **Pick your state of mind.** You've been eating because, for instance, you are lonely and want to have more intimate contact with others. You know you have to feel better about yourself as a person to do this. You know that you are an intelligent, accomplished, loving person, and you want to rekindle your belief in yourself so you can have the confidence to meet new people. State of mind: self-confidence, appreciation of your assets and your capacity for personal connection.

2. **Remember when you felt it before.** Think back to a time when you felt strong about your personal worth. Perhaps it was when you were in school working on a committee, and you pulled off a big project. Perhaps friends threw you a surprise party and you knew how loved you were. Choose one of these times and go back there in your mind, remembering as many physical details about the event, including what you did, heard, saw, and felt.

3. **Choose your anchor,** something you can use now as an association to call up the state of mind you were in at that time. It may be an object you touch or hold, such as a piece of jewelry, a small book, a photo. It could be a word or phrase you repeat to yourself that recalls that event, or a mental picture of something that happened then. It could be a sentence written on a piece of paper to take out and read.

4. **Revisit the state and use the anchor.** Go back to that positive time and experience it again. As you experience the feelings, make use of the anchor you've chosen. Look at or touch the object; think the phrase; see the picture.

5. **Test your anchor.** Come back to the present and use your anchor again. You should feel that state of mind that you are looking to re-create. (If the state is not clear or strong, try step 4 again.)

6. **Create your state.** When you're alone and about to eat, use your anchor to create your positive self-worth state of mind. Then plan to go out and get social instead. Sign up for a class, join a club or support group, call someone and make a date to go to a museum. Now you can do it.

Prep Work: Making the Goal Important

Getting into the right mindset to make changes is a powerful preparation tool. Each time you adjust your emotional behavior to amend your eating behavior, you're that much closer to a happier life. Now you need to focus on the overview: the big *goal* for which you are striving and your *commitment* to achieving this goal. Each person will have her own specific way of stating her goal. First, realize that a goal stated in the positive—what you *want*—is far easier to achieve than one stated as what you *don't want*. Then acknowledge that the goal is not the behavior; it is the outcome of behavioral changes (which make up the action stage of change). With all this in mind, and for the purposes of this book, think of the goal as "I want to eat in a healthy way, physically and emotionally, so that I will have energy and feel good about myself and my life."

Another part of preparation is to bolster your level of commitment. The more reasons you have for your goal and your commitment to reaching it, the more likely you are to succeed in reaching it, says James O. Prochaska, Ph.D., head of the Health Promotion Partnership at the University of Rhode Island and author, along with John C. Norcross, Ph.D., and Carlo C. Diclemente, Ph.D., of *Changing for Good* (William Morrow & Company). When you've thought of four or five benefits of changing your eating behavior, it may not be enough to get you to do it because there will be just as many reasons not to do it. For example, you know you'll benefit by losing weight, feeling better about yourself, having more energy, and looking better. But you also know it could be difficult, you'll feel uncomfortable with less food, your emotions may get out of control, and you'll have trouble sleeping. If however, you've found a whole lot more reasons to make the change—enough to far outweigh the excuses—your commitment will be strengthened.

Do your homework. Be an active learner. Open your mind to everything positive you think, hear, read, and see in the media about eating in a healthy way—it makes you feel more calm; it's better for your heart; your self-esteem will strengthen; you'll look better in your clothes. Make a list and let it keep growing. "Commitment based on 50 benefits rather than five will get action," says Dr. Prochaska.

Yet another way to prepare for change is to go public. By keeping your goal to yourself, you weaken your commitment. You have an easy out, an excuse not to do it. Telling people about your plan gives you yet another reason to do it. It motivates you; it stimulates your confidence. Now you're ready for action.

Action: Making the Change

Most likely you have thought about changing your behavior, desired changing your behavior, and tried to change your behavior in the past. Perhaps it didn't work because you weren't really prepared to make the change. Chapters One through Eight have armed you with an important key to increase your readiness for change—information.

▶ By better understanding the mechanism of your emotional eating, you know what you need to move away from.

▶ By choosing the strategies best suited to your particular issues, you have new behaviors to move toward.

You have also read in this chapter how to:

▶ Ready your mind for change.

▶ Focus in a positive way on your goal.

▶ Make your goal more important to you.

Now comes the action stage. This time you are prepared. You can now choose behaviors other than eating to manage your feelings. You can now head unrealistic, habitually negative emotions off at the pass. You can now practice behaviors that will strengthen your sense of self. You can now eat healthier, more moderate meals at times and in places conducive to your lifestyle. You can now ward off external overeating triggers.

While you are in this action phase of changing your behavior, there is more that you can do to bolster yourself. Dr. Prochaska suggests these reinforcements:

1. **Remind yourself of your commitment.** Some ways to do this are to say your goal aloud to yourself and/or write the statement in a diary several times a day. You should also regularly review your now long list of reasons to make the change.

2. **Enact alternative behavior.** This is called "countering," which is practicing a substitute behavior for the one you want to change. Examples are going out for a brisk walk instead of eating a bag of chips in front of the television, or having a constructive conversation with someone who made you angry instead of stuffing it down with a large meal.

3. **Make your environment change-friendly.** Let's face it, if the snack packs, chocolate bars, and French fries are not around, but fresh fruits and vegetables and whole-grain breads and crackers are, you have a much better chance of eating to feed real hunger than to feed emotions and cravings. If the tools you need for alternative behaviors, such as puzzles, art supplies, books, or walking shoes, are available, you'll be more likely to practice those behaviors.

4. **Set up a support system.** Having people around you who support and applaud your goals and changes will provide even more motivation and an arm to lean on if you should falter a bit. Find people who are genuinely on your side, whether they are a

few close friends or family members, an organized self-help group, or a trusted therapist.

5. **Reward yourself.** Treat yourself to something nice when you accomplish beneficial change. (For your purposes, this is probably not about treating yourself to a hot fudge sundae.) Go to a movie, get a manicure, take a bubble bath. Make positive statements about yourself: "I did it!" "I'm so proud of myself." And celebrate the mini-milestones of your accomplishment by rewarding yourself at the one-week or one-month mark of positive behavior. A reward system is not about bribery but about self-praise and being deserving. Rewards can be very effective positive reinforcement.

An arsenal of positive strategies has been offered in the chapters of this book, focused specifically toward particular issues. You can apply many of those tips to these five reinforcements for action.

Maintenance: Creating the Habit

Overeating is an insidious habit. When you change your behavior and practice these changes consistently for a period of time, you create a new habit. It is this period of habit development that experts in the psychology and weight-loss fields call maintenance. Maintenance is the important time that follows the action for change. The first six months to a year are when you strengthen the new habit. After that, maintenance, while still needing effort, becomes easier.

Many people who attempt lifestyle changes skip the preparation and jump right into action. Many also don't give the maintenance stage enough respect. Change works when all stages are addressed. When you give new behavior sufficient time to become habit, change can become permanent. To make this stage work for you, continue to apply the five strategies explained in the action section above: commitment, countering, environment control, support, and reward. Then be aware that temptations, triggers, and slips can undermine this stage. To deal with these issues:

▶ Be prepared for shakeups. Strength and resolve can weaken at times of emotional distress. So part of your homework for maintenance is to be ready with coping strategies for these periods. These might be the kind of solutions you would use in times of great stress, such as physical activity or deep relaxation. Extra interpersonal support helps here too.

▶ If you slip, get up and go on. Don't beat yourself up if you have a lapse or if an alternative behavior doesn't produce the desired outcome. A slip doesn't mean that you've failed or relapsed. Use the experience as a learning tool. Review the situation and examine what you did right (start with the positive aspect), what you could have done differently, and how you can do it better the next time.

Research shows that those who try but falter within a month are twice as likely to try again and succeed over the next six months as those who don't try at all.

The Choice to Change

You are a complex human being, and that is a very good thing. There are complex and myriad factors, both internal and external, that affect the way you think, feel, and behave. That, too, is a good thing. They make you the wonderfully rich and unique person you are; they are the reason there is no one else exactly like you on this earth. These factors also contribute to your relationships with everything around you, including food. Until now this may not have been such a good thing. With the help of this book, however, you now possess an understanding of the unique issues that shape the whys, hows, and whens of your eating habits. You knew before that these eating patterns are powerful. You now know that you are powerful, especially now that you are armed with the knowledge and tools to turn your eating behavior around.

You know what makes you overeat. You know what feelings, people, places, and events trigger you. You also know how to counter problem behaviors with productive ones. You know, too, how to implement a lasting change in your life. You did not develop food problems overnight, nor will you solve them, overnight. But you can solve them. Use the resources in this book and soon you will be able to say, "My history and my lifestyle may influence the way I eat, but now food does not rule my life."

Notes

Page

6 *Defined as 20 percent above an ideal or healthy weight:* G. D. Foster and Philip Kendall, "The realistic treatment of obesity: Changing the scales of success," *Clinical Psychology Review* 14 (1994), pp. 701–736.

6 *Researchers have pinpointed a so-called obesity gene in mice:* M. W. Schwartz and R. Seeley, "The new biology of body weight regulation," *Journal of the American Dietetic Association* 97 (1997), pp. 54–58.

6 *The number of taste buds you have and how sensitive they are may play a part in dictating how much:* B. J. Tepper and R. J. Nurse, "Fat perception as related to PROP taster status," *Physiological Behavior* 61 (1997), pp. 949–954.

6 *In studies of identical twins raised apart:* Foster and Kendall, op. cit., pp. 701–736.

7 *It is far from clear that the set-point idea is true for humans:* Ibid.

12 *Overweight people are no more emotionally troubled than people who are not overweight:* T. A. Wadden and A. J. Stunkard, "Social and psychological consequences of obesity," *Annals of Internal Medicine* 103 (1985), pp. 1062–1067; G. D. Foster and T. A. Wadden, "The psychology of obesity, weight loss and weight regain: Research and clinical findings," in G. L. Blackburn and B. S. Kanders (eds.), *Obesity: PathoPhysiology, Psychology and Treatment* (Chapman and Hall, 1994), pp. 140–166.

Page

13 *Falling off a diet only to overeat or binge as a reaction to deprivation:* J. Rodin, *Body Traps* (Quill, William Morrow, 1992), p. 183.

16 *5 percent of adolescent and adult women and 1 percent of men have:* American Anorexia and Bulimia Association, New York City, 1997.

17 *BED is defined as:* R. H. Kuehnel and T. A. Wadden, "Binge eating disorder, weight cycling, and psychopathology," *International Journal of Eating Disorders* 15 (1994), pp. 321–329.

17 *It is estimated that as many as one to two million Americans and 10 to 15 percent of overweight people:* American Anorexia and Bulimia Association.

17 *"Problem eaters"; "non-bingers":* Kuehnel and Wadden, op. cit., pp. 321–329.

18 *An extreme form of this behavior:* C. S. Rand, A. M. Macgregor, and A. J. Stunkard, "The night eating syndrome in the general population and among postoperative obesity surgery patients," *International Journal of Eating Disorders* 22 (1997), pp. 65–69.

19 *In 1989 Richard M. Ganley reviewed 30 years of studies:* R. M. Ganley, "Emotion and eating in obesity: A review of the literature," *International Journal of Eating Disorders* 8 (1989), pp. 343–361.

20 *Why carbohydrates? Because, the research suggests, for some people they help the brain produce more serotonin:* J. J. Wurtman et al., "Carbohydrate craving in obese people: Suppression by treatment affecting serotoninergic transmission," *International Journal of Eating Disorders* 1 (1981), pp. 2–15.

21 *Often overweight people overreport emotional eating as a result of a societal expectation:* D. B. Allison, S. Heshka, "Emotion and eating in obesity? A critical analysis," *International Journal of Eating Disorders* 13 (1993), pp. 289–295.

34 *Seeking relief from some intense emotions, maybe anger, guilt, or extreme anxiety:* V. M. Lingswiler, J. H. Crowther, and M.A.P. Stephens, "Emotional reactivity and eating in binge eating and obesity," *Journal of Behavioral Medicine* 10 (1987), pp. 287–299.

Page

44 *Differences in how mothers with varying concerns about their own weight act while feeding their babies:* Rodin, op. cit., pp. 35–36.

48 *Studies show that when they're fed more than usual at one meal or snack time, kids will usually compensate:* S. L. Johnson, and L. L. Birch, "Parents' and children's adiposity and eating style," *Pediatrics* 94 (1994), pp. 653–661.

49 *The many ways that parents try to control their child's eating behavior can make it difficult for the child:* E .M. Satter, "Internal regulation and the evolution of normal growth as the basis for prevention of obesity in children," *Journal of the American Dietetic Association* 96 (1996), pp. 860–864.

65 *Research shows that this body image/self-concept connection starts at a young age:* G. W. Guyot, L. Fairchild, and M. Hill, "Physical fitness, sport participation, body build and self-concept of elementary school children," *International Journal of Sports Psychology* 12 (1981), pp. 105–116.

67 *Self-denial wears a person down, causing ego depletion leading to a weakening of willpower:* R. F. Baumeister et al., "Ego depletion: Is the active self a limited resource?" *Journal of Personality and Social Psychology* 74 (1998), pp. 1252–1265.

67 *Subjects who experienced dieting weight fluctuations over the course of a year exhibited more signs of depression, stress, and low self-esteem:* J. P. Foreyt et al., "Psychological correlates of weight fluctuation," *International Journal of Eating Disorders* 17 (1995), pp. 263–275.

69 *67 percent of lifetime members overall, and 37 percent who'd been lifetime members for five years or more, had maintained their weight:* G. Christakis and K. Miller-Kovach, "Maintenance of weight goal among Weight Watchers lifetime members," *Nutrition Today* 31 (1996), pp. 29–31.

69 *An effective program of weight management should combine* moderate *changes in food intake and activity:* Foster and Kendall, op. cit., pp. 701–736.

69 *In fact, overweight is a condition that may be the most stigmatized by society:* J. Crocker, B. Cornwell, and B. Major, "The stigma of overweight: Affective consequences of attributional ambiguity," *Journal of Personality and Social Psychology* 64 (1993), pp. 60–70.

Page

70 *Again, compulsive overeating or bingeing may be used to escape from this negative self-related feeling:* Ibid.

76 *Psychologists agree that caring for your body can help you foster a steady sense of security:* Rodin, op. cit., pp. 54 and 70.

77 *Studies show that those who have social support are better able to keep weight off than those who don't:* S. Kayman, W. Bruvold, and J. S. Stern, "Maintenance and relapse after weight loss in women: Behavioral aspects," *American Journal of Clinical Nutrition* 52 (1990), pp. 800–807; J. P. Foreyt and G. K. Goodrick, "Factors common to successful treatment for the obese patient," *Medicine and Science in Sports and Exercise* 23 (1991), 292–297.

89 *Some depressed people who remove caffeine and sugar from their diets experience greater energy and improved mood:* L. Christensen, "Effects of eating behavior on mood: A review of the literature," *International Journal of Eating Disorders* 14 (1993), pp. 171–183; L. Christensen, "The effect of carbohydrates on affect," *Nutrition* 13 (1997), pp. 503–514.

92 *Exposure to intense, full-spectrum light for one or two hours a day or less:* T. Partonen, "Effects of morning light treatment of subjective sleepiness and mood in winter depression," *Journal of Affective Disorders* 30 (1994), pp. 47–56.

103 *Women may have a tougher time with stress eating than men:* N. Grunberg and R. Straub, "The role of gender and taste class in the effects of stress on eating," *Health Psychology* 11 (1992), pp. 97–100.

110 *The physical stress response, which includes elevated heart rate and blood sugar, seems to suppress aspects of the immune system:* R. S. Elliot, M.D., *From Stress to Strength: How to Lighten Your Load and Save Your Life* (Bantam, 1984), pp. 22–29.

116 *Some studies report that 20 to 40 percent of all women in this country are compulsive eaters:* R. H. Striegel-Moore, L. R. Silberstein, and J. Rodin, "Toward an understanding of risk factors for bulimia," *American Psychologist* 41 (1986), pp. 246–263.

Page

116 *As a person who's in the habit of controlling food intake, you probably don't respond to internal hunger cues:* Interview with Janet Polivy, University of Toronto.

128 *Anger should be considered both as a variable emotional state that comes and goes and as a personality trait:* C. D. Spielberger, G. Jacobs, S. Russell, and R. Crane, "Assessment of anger: The state-trait anger scale," in J. N. Butcher and C. D. Spielberger (eds.), *Advances in Personality Assessment*, vol. 2 (Erlbaum, 1983), pp. 161–189.

128 *Studies of twins suggest:* S. P. Thomas (ed.), *Women and Anger.* Report of the Women's Anger Study, University of Tennessee, Knoxville. (Springer, 1993), p. 41.

131 *Research has consistently shown that trait anger:* Ibid., pp. 219–220.

131 *From the 18th century through the mid-19th century, men, women, and children:* Ibid., p. 45.

145 *Pioneering researcher Frieda Fromm-Reichman described loneliness as "the longing for interpersonal intimacy":* F. Fromm-Reichman, "Loneliness," *Psychiatry* 22 (1959), pp. 1–15.

149 *Says Stanford University School of Medicine mind-body researcher Kenneth R. Pelletier, M.D.:* K. R. Pelletier, *Sound Mind, Sound Body* (Simon & Schuster, 1994), p. 149.

164 *It is the way you are thinking, feeling, and then reacting physically:* J. O'Connor and J. Seymour, *Introducing NLP—Neuro-linguistic Programming* (Aquarian Press, 1990), p. 49.

165 *It is a way that you can, whenever you choose, trigger yourself into a state of mind:* Ibid., pp. 53–55.

168 *The more reasons you have for your goal and your commitment to reaching it:* Interview with James Prochaska, University of Rhode Island, 1996.

Index